The Great God Pan

The History of His Cult

John Kruse

GREEN MAGIC

Green Magic
53 Brooks Road
Street
Somerset
BA16 0PP
England
www.greenmagicpublishing.com

Designed and typeset by K.DESIGN
Winscombe, Somerset

ISBN 9781838132453

GREEN MAGIC

Contents

Preface

The idea for this book first occurred to me when working on my study of the history of nymphs, *Nymphology*.[1] Throughout my research, I was aware of the presence of Pan, as well as his entourage of fauns and satyrs, in the background, pursuing and copulating with those woodland nymphs.

These observations chimed with the knowledge that certain early twentieth century writers with whom I was familiar, such as Arthur Machen, Algernon Blackwood and Kenneth Grahame, had written about 'the Great God Pan.' I was intrigued by this revived cult of Pan and set about my investigations. I was led through many strange byways of literature, philosophy and art. This book is the result of my wanderings in search of answers to puzzled questions: why did late Victorian society revert to a reverence for the goat-god Pan? Were they serious about this devotion and what did they hope to derive from it? Why, today, do so few know about this, outside of some specialists in English literature?

One of the most accessible books on this theme from this period is Kenneth Grahame's *Wind in the Willows*. Many people will read its curiously elegiac episode in which the river creatures meet the

---

1   *Nymphology – A Brief History of Nymphs,2020.*

god Pan, but will not appreciate that this chapter is not a strange one-off, but is evidence of a much wider fascination with the Greek God. This book tries to put this incident in Grahame's book into its wider cultural context.

PART ONE

Background

The 'cult of Pan' that emerged into British literature and art in the later nineteenth century was by no means isolated or unique. It originated (plainly) from the ancient cult of the Mediterranean in the classical period, but the memories of Pan did not leap suddenly across centuries to fill the imaginations of Victorian era writers and painters. Rather, there was a continual thread of learning about, and celebration of, the god that connected Imperial Rome to the British Empire.

The next three chapters survey how the embers of the cult were kept smouldering over a millennium.

CHAPTER 1

In Arcady

"Beloved Pan, and all ye other gods who haunt this place!"[2]

My interest in this book is the recent cultural history of Pan: his meaning to painters and writers over the last two hundred years or so. Nevertheless, it is necessary to sketch out a little of his background before we see how the classical god and his mythology were used by the Victorians and Edwardians.

Pan is a pastoral god of ancient Greece; he originated in the mountainous region of Arcadia in the Peloponnese peninsula. His name derives from a word for 'pasturer' but, from a very early date, it was also interpreted as meaning 'all' or 'universal,' considerably boosting his potential significance as a deity.

There are several accounts of Pan's parentage. According to one, his father is Hermes and his mother a forest nymph called Penelope. A second version says that he was the son of Zeus and the nymph Calisto and a third recounts that his father was Mercury and his mother, Dryope (another nymph). All in all, there are fourteen different versions of Pan's conception, but what is

---

2 *Phaedrus.*

agreed in all of them is that his mother rejected him because of his ugliness – the fact that his lower half was that of a hairy goat, his upper half human, yet still surmounted by horns. By way of contrast, it is said that Pan's father, Mercury, was so delighted by his grotesque appearance that he took his son to Olympus to amuse the other gods. This status as a mocked outsider is something that proved to be a significant part of his character for later generations.

Pan's separation from his mother naturally affected the young deity and he became an inveterate pursuer of nymphs throughout his adult life, although, in some accounts, he had a loving relationship with a single nymph, Pitys. Certainly, it is Pan as nymphophile that will be a particular focus in this study.

Pan is vigorous and lustful; he is a giver of fertility. His main concern is with the health and wellbeing of flocks and herds, but he can also inspire sudden terrors, or 'panics,' amongst the grazing livestock, causing them to stampede. Pan can send visions and dreams to humans and he was reported, in ancient times, to act as an oracle on Mount Lycaeus.

Pan became a god of mountains and forests, the companion of shepherds and inventor of the reed pipes, following his unsuccessful pursuit of the nymph Syrinx, who was one of Diana's retinue and, therefore, sworn to chastity. Later, he joined Dionysus' band and became associated with the bacchanalian cult of that divinity. Dionysus' wine and Pan's music (as well as his fondness for noise and chaos) meant that the gods' followers were associated with ecstatic rites involving sex and wild celebration. In ancient times their cult attracted many followers – until it was banned by the Roman Emperor Commodus in 186 AD.

In fact, this suppression during the second century only seemed to confirm an already existing rumour that had been circulating in the ancient world since the reign of the Roman Emperor Tiberius

(14–37 AD). According to the writer Plutarch, a man called Thamus, who was steersman on a ship sailing to Italy by way of the island of Paxi in the Ionian Sea, thrice heard a voice call out to him that "the Great Pan is dead." The phrase became very well known and was the subject of much speculation and interpretation. We shall hear it again later in this book; suffice to say though, Pan had not died, he was not forgotten and his worship did not disappear completely.[3]

Several other minor classical divinities are closely related to Pan and are often mentioned (or pictured) interchangeably with him. Firstly, there is Aegipan, which means 'Goat-Pan.' According to some ancient authorities, he was a deity distinct from Pan, whilst others treated them as identical. Some texts claim he was a son of Zeus and became a constellation. Greek scholar Eratosthenes stated that Aegipan was Pan's father and that both had bodies that were half-goat and half-fish. Roman author Plutarch recorded an old story that Aegipan was the child of incest and was the same as Silvanus, the God of Woods and Waste Places.

Secondly, in Greek mythology, the satyrs are minor deities or spirits who are also half-beast, half-man. In the earliest representations, the satyrs had horses' tails, but they came to be seen more and more like Pan, with goats' ears, horns and tail. Just like him, they loved wine, women and song and could strike fear into country folk. The satyrs are often depicted playing flutes and dancing with nymphs and were often found in the company of the god Bacchus, the God of Vines. Some view Pan as the leader of the satyrs.

Faunus was an ancient rural deity in Italy, whose function was to make crops and livestock fruitful. He was associated with the

---

3   Plutarch, *On the Obsolescence of Oracles*, V, 17.

fates and was believed to have prophetic powers. Growing Greek influence upon Latin culture saw Faunus increasingly identified with Pan, but he was also linked to Silvanus (see earlier). Fauns as a class were minor nature deities who tended to be treated as the same as the Greek satyrs.

Finally, there is Silenus, who was said to be the son of Hermes (or Pan) and of a nymph. He became the companion and substitute parent of Dionysus and he was often imagined as a fat, jolly man drinking wine in the company of satyrs. Whilst often intoxicated (or, perhaps, because of this), Silenus was also said to be able to see into the future. In fact, the *silenoi* (plural) could just be an alternative name for a particular sub-group of satyrs.

This brief summary outlines the key aspects of Pan and those other minor divinities associated with him. Overwhelmingly, he was seen positively. He was associated with fecundity and with pleasure. His knowledge of the future, even if there was no control over events to come, at least enabled his followers to prepare for what was ahead. Primarily, Pan was about an unbridled indulgence and natural, simple enjoyment. There was much to recommend him to future generations.

CHAPTER 2

Renaissance Revival

"Pan is a God, Apollo is no more!"[4]

The Greek myths and stories were never forgotten, but in the Christian culture of the Middle Ages in Europe, they were not given great attention. The revival of classical learning known as the Renaissance, which began in the early fifteenth century, made more Greek and Roman texts available than had been the case, as well as creating a spirit of philosophical enquiry that made Western societies more open to these rediscovered materials. A familiarity with the texts and with the heroes and gods and goddesses of the ancient classical world became the hallmark of a cultured person. Across Europe, knowledge of Latin and Greek came to form the basis of a 'good' education, as in the English establishment of 'grammar' schools. The young scholars attending these were not learning the proper usage of

---

4   John Lyly, *Midas*, c.1590, Act IV, scene 1.

English, but becoming adept in the declension of nouns and the conjugation of verbs in Latin.

I have discussed before the impact of this new learning upon British conceptions of their native mythology and how fairies, elves, hobgoblins and mermaids easily became synonymous with nymphs, satyrs and sirens. The god Pan, of course, was one element in that wholesale importation of intertwined stories and characters.[5]

The English poet John Fletcher (1579–1625) was, for instance, inspired to write an entire play, *The Faithful Shepherdess*, that focussed upon the god. In particular it includes a *Hymn to Pan*, in which the Arcadian god is praised and all the aspects of his character that were described in the previous chapter are mentioned:

> "Sing his praises that doth keep
> Our flocks from harm.
> Pan, the father of our sheep;
> And arm in arm
> Tread we softly in a round,
> Whilst the hollow neighbouring ground
> Fills the music with her sound.
>
> Pan, O great god Pan, to thee
> Thus do we sing!
> Thou who keep'st us chaste and free
> As the young spring:
> Ever be thy honour spoke
> From that place the morn is broke
> To that place day doth unyoke!"[6]

---

5   See, for example, my *British Fairies* (2017) or *Fayerie* (2020).
6   From *The Faithful Shepherdess*, c.1609, Act I, scene 1.

In fact, throughout the play, there are invocations of 'Shepherd Pan' and 'Great Pan,' asking him to speed the plough and bless the flocks. Pan is called upon for aid and oaths are sworn in his name: "By the dawning of the day,/ By the power of night and Pan." Pan is a constant presence in the play, spoken of but not seen, and he is attended by his troop of satyrs, fauns *and fairies*, all of whom wield magical powers.[7]

At one point a satyr appears and discloses his orders from the god:

> "Now whilst the moon doth rule the sky,
>   And the stars, whose feeble light
>   Give a pale shadow to the night,
>   Are up, great Pan commanded me
>   To walk this grove about, whilst he
>   In a corner of the wood,
>   Where never mortal foot hath stood,
>   Keeps dancing, music and a feast,
>   To entertain a lovely guest:
>   Where he gives her many a rose
>   Sweeter than the breath that blows
>   The leaves: grapes, berries of the best,
>   I never saw so great a feast."[8]

Whilst Pan is engaged with Syrinx, the satyr's mission is to act as a will of the wisp (a "flaming fire") to lead humans back to the paths they have lost and to protect virgins from assaults upon their virtue by mustering the fairies to pinch the potential rapist "until

---

7   Act III, scene 1.
8   Act III, scene 1.

all his lustful thoughts are gone." Here, it has to be said, the goat god seems to be issuing instructions that run entirely against his true nature.

For Fletcher, Pan was closely associated with music and dancing (much like the British fairies were). The same pastimes are seen too in John Milton's *Lycidas:*

> "Meanwhile, the rural ditties were not mute,
> Temper'd to the oaten flute;
> Rough satyrs danc'd and fauns with cloven heel,
> From the glad sound would not be absent long."

Ben Jonson also made use of classical deities in his work. His royal *Entertainment at Althorp* of 1603, also called *The Satyr,* featured the satyr alongside Queen Mab and a company of fairies. A year later, he wrote a further masque for the king and queen, the *Entertainment at Highgate,* which is also known as *The Penates,* and which features Pan alongside Mercury and other classical figures.

Needless to say, Fletcher, Milton and Jonson hadn't suddenly forsaken the Church of England and become pagans. These works were displays of style and learning and, indeed, it might be better to think rather of the conversion (or, at least, co-option) of the Greek gods into English folklore. Writing about witchcraft in 1584, Reginald Scot listed all the bogies and other imaginary beings used by parents to scare children:

> "But in our childhood our mother's maids have so terrified
> us with… elves… fairies, satyrs, pans, fauns, sylvans…
> centaurs… nymphs… and other bugs, that we are afraid of
> our own shadows."[9]

---

9   Scot, *The Discovery of Witchcraft,* Book VII, chapter 15.

As can be seen, the classical beings are mixed in with a much longer list of traditional sprites, plainly treating them as equivalent – if not identical. The same approach can be seen in Thomas Hobbes' *Leviathan*, where he observed how the 'Gentiles' (pagans) had once "filled almost all places with spirits called demons: the plains with Pans and Satyrs; the woods with Fauns and Nymphs, and a whole kingdom of fairies and bugbears." Robert Burton too showed no hesitation in lumping together classical and British spirits: "Terrestrial devils are those *lares*, Genii, Fauns, Satyrs, Wood-nymphs... Fairies, Robin Goodfellows etc."[10]

Indeed, pipe-playing Pan simply became musician at the fairies' revels, supplanting Tom Thumb who had previously played on his fiddle for them. Playwright Jasper Fisher in 1633 described how "Pan doth play care away,/ Fayries small... Dance around on the ground." Four decades later, this role was well enough known to be alluded to in popular ballads:

> "Each Shepherdess around
> Fairy ground does dance
> While Pan does pipe and sing."[11]

Lastly, in 1612, William Warner published the second part of his *Albion's England*, a history of the English realm. Incorporated within this was an episode entitled 'The Shepherd's Dream,' in which the pastoralist falls asleep on a green bank and witnesses a conclave of fairy spirits. He sees "Fairie-Elves" dancing in a

---

10 Hobbes, *Leviathan*, 1651, Part One c.XII; see too c.II; see also Burton, *Anatomy of Melancholy*, section II(2), *A Digression of the Nature of Spirits, Bad Angels, or Devils and how they Cause Melancholy*.

11 Fisher, *Fuimus Troes, – Aeneid II, The True Trojans*, 1633, Act I, scene 5, 'Song;' 'Beauteous Jenny,' 1672–96.

circle with "Larrs of another kind" (a Larr is a Roman domestic spirit, akin to the British brownie, which Warner probably means). Robin Goodfellow then joins the company and laments the changes that have taken place in English society over the previous century. The world has changed, he complains: the monks and friars are gone and Great Pan's great vicar (the Pope) is no longer obeyed. Here, of course, Pan is used as another name for the devil and it is true to observe that the hoofed and horned appearance of Pan had contributed greatly to the Church's image of Satan over preceding centuries. However, by the early seventeenth century, as Fletcher demonstrated, writers were more prepared to reassess these prejudices and to deal with Pan on his own terms. It might be added that amongst the other works of Warner are a translation of the *Menæchmi* by Plautus (1595) and a collection of prose tales entitled *Pan his Syrinx, or Pipe, Compact of Seven Reedes* (1584). This only serves to underline the status of classical knowledge at the period.

In short, Pan had become not just part of the mental furniture of every cultured individual, but had been incorporated into the fabric of English folk tradition.

CHAPTER 3

Romantic Pan

Towards the close of the eighteenth century, antiquarian interest in Pan began to revive among liberal scholars. For example, in his *Discourse on the Worship of Priapus* (1786), Richard Payne-Knight treated the god as "the principle of universal order," creator and prime component of the cosmos. Pan represented matter animated by the divine spirit and was symbolised by water and by light. The dances associated with Pan represented the movement of the Universe. The creative power of sexuality was symbolised by the pairing of satyrs and nymphs.

During the same period, a group of Gloucestershire gentry, led by Benjamin Hyett, almost put Payne-Knight's theories into practice. They organised an annual procession through the Cotswold village of Painswick, in which a statue of the deity was carried aloft to public acclaim. With some interruptions, this ceremony continued until it was suppressed in 1950 and the statute was buried (later it was recovered and put up in the garden of a large house). Perhaps it is more than coincidence that, a century and a half after Hyett, the author and playwright James Elroy Flecker celebrated the presence of Pan in the Gloucestershire landscape with these lines:

"Have I not sat on Painswick Hill
　With a nymph upon my knees,
　And she as rosy as the dawn,
　And naked as the breeze?"[12]

It seems clear from these two examples that, two hundred years on from the English Renaissance, there had been no diminution in the English love of the classics. The Romantic poets of the late eighteenth and early nineteenth centuries were just as familiar with the Greek myths as their predecessors – and just as inclined to employ that knowledge in their verse.

In 1820, Shelley composed a *Hymn of Pan*, for example. The song was intended to form part of Mary Shelley's verse play *Midas* and it conjured the god's aspect as a poet and musician, albeit with a tragic tone:

"From the forests and highlands
　We come, we come;
　From the river-girt islands,
　Where loud waves are dumb
　Listening to my sweet pipings.
　The wind in the reeds and the rushes,
　The bees on the bells of thyme,
　The birds on the myrtle bushes,
　The cicale above in the lime,
　And the lizards below in the grass,
　Were as silent as ever old Tmolus was,
　Listening to my sweet pipings.

12　Flecker, *Oak & Olive*.

Liquid Peneus was flowing,
And all dark Tempe lay
In Pelion's shadow, outgrowing
The light of the dying day,
Speeded by my sweet pipings.
The Sileni, and Sylvans, and Fauns,
And the Nymphs of the woods and the waves,
To the edge of the moist river-lawns,
And the brink of the dewy caves,
And all that did then attend and follow,
Were silent with love, as you now, Apollo,
With envy of my sweet pipings.

I sang of the dancing stars,
I sang of the daedal [curious] Earth,
And of Heaven, and the giant wars,
And Love, and Death, and Birth—
And then I chang'd my pipings,
Singing how down the vale of Maenalus
I pursu'd a maiden and clasp'd a reed.
Gods and men, we are all deluded thus!
It breaks in our bosom and then we bleed.
All wept, as I think both ye now would,
If envy or age had not frozen your blood,
At the sorrow of my sweet pipings."

The great poet of the period who was most constantly inspired by classical sources was John Keats. We know of the effect upon him of his reading of George Chapman's *Homer* (1816) and also of the influence of William Wordsworth's own treatment of the Greek mythology in *The Excursion* (1814), as revealed in the lines which follow:

"Once more to distant Ages of the world
    Let us revert, and place before our thoughts
    The face which rural Solitude might wear
    To the unenlightened Swains of pagan Greece.
    – In that fair Clime, the lonely Herdsman, stretched
    On the soft grass through half a summer's day,
    With music lulled his indolent repose:
    And, in some fit of weariness, if he,
    When his own breath was silent, chanced to hear
    A distant strain, far sweeter than the sounds
    Which his poor skill could make, his Fancy fetched,
    Even from the blazing Chariot of the Sun,
    A beardless Youth, who touched a golden lute,
    And filled the illumined groves with ravishment.
    The nightly Hunter, lifting up his eyes
    Towards the crescent Moon, with grateful heart
    Called on the lovely wanderer who bestowed
    That timely light, to share his joyous sport:
    And hence, a beaming Goddess with her Nymphs,
    Across the lawn and through the darksome grove,
    (Not unaccompanied with tuneful notes
    By echo multiplied from rock or cave)
    Swept in the storm of chase, as Moon and Stars
    Glance rapidly along the clouded heavens,
    When winds are blowing strong. The Traveller slaked
    His thirst from Rill or gushing Fount, and thanked
    The Naiad. -Sunbeams, upon distant Hills
    Gliding apace, with Shadows in their train,
    Might, with small help from fancy, be transformed

Into fleet Oreads sporting visibly.
The Zephyrs, fanning as they passed, their wings,
Lacked not, for love, fair Objects, whom they wooed
With gentle whisper. Withered Boughs grotesque,
Stripped of their leaves and twigs by hoary age,
From depth of shaggy covert peeping forth
In the low vale, or on steep mountain side;
And, sometimes, intermixed with stirring horns
Of the live Deer, or Goat's depending beard;
These were the lurking Satyrs, a wild brood
Of gamesome Deities! or Pan himself,
The simple Shepherd's awe-inspiring God."[13]

Indeed, many years earlier, in *The Prelude* (1799), Wordsworth had already demonstrated his awareness of the essential attributes of the goat god:

"Of Pan, Invisible God, thrilling the rocks
With tutelary music, from all harm
The fold protecting."[14]

Wordsworth's close friend and associate, Samuel Taylor Coleridge, also displayed a keen understanding of the nature and power of the Arcadian deity's myth. For a few years he had described himself as a pantheist (as too did Wordsworth, who sought to find the supernatural in the natural world) and he wrote perceptively that the Greeks had chosen their image of the god for very good reasons. For them, it represented "the mixture of the human and

---

13 *The Excursion*, Book IV, lines 840–81.
14 *Prelude*, Book VIII,

the brute form in the figure, by which they realised the idea of their mysterious Pan, as representing intelligence blended with a darker power, deeper, mightier, and more universal than the conscious intellect of man; than intelligence."[15]

During his short literary career, John Keats was to write about Apollo, Endymion, Hyperion and many other figures from Greek mythology. Amongst these, he composed a hymn to 'the great god Pan,' calling upon him, in part as the giver of fruitfulness and friend of shepherds, but in part too as a good-natured player of tricks (just like the British Puck or Robin Goodfellow) who also grants visions of the future:

"Hear us, great Pan!

O thou, for whose soul-soothing quiet, turtles
Passion their voices cooingly 'mong myrtles,
What time thou wanderest at eventide
Through sunny meadows, that outskirt the side
Of thine enmossed realms: O thou, to whom
Broad leaved fig trees even now foredoom
Their ripen'd fruitage; yellow girted bees
Their golden honeycombs; our village leas
Their fairest-blossom'd beans and poppied corn;
The chuckling linnet its five young unborn,
To sing for thee; low creeping strawberries
Their summer coolness; pent up butterflies
Their freckled wings; yea, the fresh budding year
All its completions – be quickly near,

---

15 Coleridge, *Biographia Literaria*, 1817, c.21, 'Remarks on the present mode of conducting critical journals.'

By every wind that nods the mountain pine,
O forester divine!

Thou, to whom every fawn and satyr flies
For willing service; whether to surprise
The squatted hare while in half sleeping fit;
Or upward ragged precipices flit
To save poor lambkins from the eagle's maw;
Or by mysterious enticement draw
Bewildered shepherds to their path again;
Or to tread breathless round the frothy main,
And gather up all fancifullest shells
For thee to tumble into Naiads' cells,
And, being hidden, laugh at their out-peeping;
Or to delight thee with fantastic leaping,
The while they pelt each other on the crown
With silvery oak apples, and fir cones brown-
By all the echoes that about thee ring,
Hear us, O satyr king!

O Hearkener to the loud clapping shears,
While ever and anon to his shorn peers
A ram goes bleating: Winder of the horn,
When snouted wild-boars routing tender corn
Anger our huntsman: Breather round our farms,
To keep off mildews, and all weather harms:
Strange ministrant of undescribed sounds,
That come a swooning over hollow grounds,
And wither drearily on barren moors:
Dread opener of the mysterious doors
Leading to universal knowledge – see,

Great son of Dryope,
The many that are come to pay their vows
With leaves about their brows!

Be still the unimaginable lodge
For solitary thinkings; such as dodge
Conception to the very bourne of heaven,
Then leave the naked brain: be still the leaven,
That spreading in this dull and clodded earth
Gives it a touch ethereal – a new birth:
Be still a symbol of immensity;
A firmament reflected in a sea;
An element filling the space between;
An unknown – but no more: we humbly screen
With uplift hands our foreheads, lowly bending,
And giving out a shout most heaven rending,
Conjure thee to receive our humble Paean,
Upon thy Mount Lycean!"[16]

For Keats, this Pan is the source of poetic inspiration – the 'leaven' that gives a 'touch ethereal' to mortal men – as well as a symbol of the vastness of nature.

Finally, it might be added that Keats' absorption in the myths of Greece extended to a love of nymphs, which he shared with Pan. 'Nymphs,' in the prosaic sense of easy-going country girls, feature in several of his poems, but they are also present as muses. In *Sleep and Poetry*, he highlights Pan's particular significance to him – as a bringer of poetic inspiration – and he then proceeds to lay out his artistic plan:

---

16   Keats, *Endimion*, Book I, lines 256–306.

"O, for ten years, that I may overwhelm
  Myself in poesy! so I may do the deed
  That my own soul has to itself decreed.
  Then I will pass the countries that I see
  In long perspective, and continually
  Taste their pure fountains. First the realm I'll pass
  Of Flora, and old Pan: sleep in the grass,
  Feed upon apples red, and strawberries,
  And choose each pleasure that my fancy sees;
  Catch the white-handed nymphs in shady places,
  To woo sweet kisses from averted faces—
  Play with their fingers, touch their shoulders white
  Into a pretty shrinking with a bite
  As hard as lips can make it: till, agreed,
  A lovely tale of human life we'll read."

Likewise, Keats' 1817 poem *To Leigh Hunt Esq.* lies at the same intersection of Pan, poesy and pretty nymphs:

"Glory and loveliness have passed away;
  For if we wander out in early morn,
  No wreathed incense do we see upborne
  Into the east, to meet the smiling day:
  No crowd of nymphs soft voic'd and young, and gay,
  In woven baskets bringing ears of corn,
  Roses, and pinks, and violets, to adorn
  The shrine of Flora in her early May.
  But there are left delights as high as these,
  And I shall ever bless my destiny,
  That in a time, when under pleasant trees
  Pan is no longer sought, I feel a free

A leafy luxury, seeing I could please
With these poor offerings, a man like thee."

Keats' *Ode to Psyche* encapsulates the nymph's sensuous nature when he stumbles upon the fair nymph and her lover Cupid, asleep in each other's embrace on a bed of grass. She is addressed as "latest born and loveliest vision far/ Of all Olympus' faded hierarchy," worn out by loving but "ready still past kisses to outnumber." He promises to build her shrine of verse, where "moss-lain Dryads shall be lulled to sleep" and whose windows shall be left open at night "to let the warm love in!" Keats expanded upon the kisses shared by Psyche and Cupid in *I Stood Tip-Toe Upon a Little Hill*, composed in December 1816. He compares the couple's joy, ravishment and wonder to that felt by one who:

"…who pull'd the boughs aside,
That we might look into a forest wide,
To catch a glimpse of Fawns, and Dryades
Coming with softest rustle through the trees;
And garlands woven of flowers wild, and sweet,
Upheld on ivory wrists, or sporting feet:
Telling us how fair, trembling Syrinx fled
Arcadian Pan, with such a fearful dread.
Poor nymph, – poor Pan, – how he did weep to find,
Nought but a lovely sighing of the wind
Along the reedy stream; a half-heard strain,
Full of sweet desolation – balmy pain."

With these final lines, we have gone full circle and return to Pan, now viewed as the unrequited lover – not the potential molester of maidens, but a true suitor rejected.

For the Romantics, Pan was known to be a rural god of flocks and shepherds, but his greatest significance was as a fount or facilitator of poetry.[17] In this respect, he was a refined deity, scarcely goaty at all...

17 See too Victor Hugo, *Pan*, 1831.

PART TWO

The Modern Cult of Pan

As I have indicated, from the early nineteenth century onwards, artists and writers began to derive increasing inspiration from the imagery and symbolism of the goat god. He was found to be a multi-dimensional deity, fecund with wisdom about a wide range of aspects of life.

As we shall see, Pan suddenly blossomed into a cult in both senses of the word: there was renewed religious enthusiasm, but he also became fashionable amongst the cultured elite. References to the woodland deity, both detailed and superficial, became popular exactly because they had a modish currency.

A ready example of this may be J. M. Barrie's play and stories concerning *Peter Pan*. There is precious little in this of the Greek god, other than a sense of Peter being an outsider, only part human (and part bird) and an uncivilised, uneducated child of nature. Arthur Rackham's illustration of *Peter Pan in Kensington Gardens* shows him as an ordinary human baby – confessedly, in one place playing pan-pipes which he has made from reeds.[18]

What the revival certainly showed was that Pan was not dead at all, simply dormant. Max Beerbohm had proposed the same, too, suggesting that the ancient gods still existed amongst us in disguise, merely waiting for the time when they could cast off their disguises and rule over mankind again.[19] In any case, for some people the god's demise had all been pretence anyway: Lord Dunsany, for example, in *The Death of Pan*, has the goat god bounding away when some women laugh at his apparent corpse laid out, stiff and still. In *The Tomb of Pan*, which concludes the same collection of stories, Pan mocks the people who have constructed a huge tomb for him, "that the dreadful worship of long ago may be remembered and avoided by all." The builders think that this

---

18 Barrie, *Peter Pan in Kensington Gardens*, 1906, c.2.
19 Beerbohm, 'Hellas via Bradfield,' June 23rd 1900,
      collected in *Recreations and Reflections*, 1902.

"infamous god" and his "wicked age" have passed away; he laughs at their error.[20]

The reason for the revival of Pan in the later nineteenth century was that he stood as a symbol for an alternative to modern, Western society. Greek pantheism was attractive because its multiplicity seemed to have the potential to reflect the complexity of humanity better than the inherited monotheism of Judaeo-Christianity.[21] As for Pan, because his name could be interpreted (incorrectly, as we've seen) to mean 'all,' he could assume the role of a universal god of nature. His half-goat aspect, which had formerly made him seem rather ignorant and brutish, now became a more abstract virtue. By his dual nature, Pan was not one of the cold Olympian gods; instead, he was vibrant and vital, an all-pervasive force who reigned over the natural world.

Pan offered the late Victorians and Edwardians a number of facets that were valuable and useful. Despite some attempts to revive ancient British paganism through the order of the druids, traditional British myths and folklore didn't offer the same coherence and scope as the Greek mythology, which was so much more familiar to many from their schooldays. Pan, of all that pantheon, may

---

20 In Dunsany, *Fifty-One Tales,* 1915.
21 See James Hillman, *Pan & the Nightmare,* 1972.

have been alien and anachronistic, but he was also unencumbered by too many stories and associations (unlike the rest of the ancient pantheon); he stood to some degree outside the dense web of incidents and relationships that made up the classical myths. Pan was malleable; he could be shaped to contemporary, British needs – and what was needed, it seemed, was an ambiguous god for an ambiguous age.

As the nineteenth century drew to a close, Britain seemed to enter a period of considerable political and social transition; old certainties became unstable and doubtful. Scientific developments, such as the theory of evolution, and geological and palaeontological discoveries, had undermined the formerly unquestioned veracity of the Bible. A second wave of Industrial Revolution brought accelerating technological change. The global and military predominance of the British Empire was beginning to seem less secure as new states, such as Germany, became more assertive. Social and sexual revolution was brewing and individuals sought a new spirituality. For some, that seemed to lie in arts and culture through the Aesthetic Movement; others romanticised the rural past and the medieval sense of community (the Pre-Raphaelites, William Morris and others). This nostalgia for a (possibly imaginary) past that was closer to nature is, it could be argued, a key part of the British psyche, but during the period we're discussing, it was already starting to fade when the Great War smashed any lingering illusions to bits.[22]

Yet others turned to the neo-paganism we are discussing here. Pan was placed at the forefront of this revival in Victorian England. The animal and sexual aspects of his persona, which had been problematic previously, now highlighted the defects of the morality of the time when contrasted to the Greeks' concerns with their senses and sexuality and their openness to pleasure.

Pan was contradictory, ambivalent and equivocal, a god ideally suited to an age that both sought and feared the future, reminisced for and rejected the past. As a deity, he could be seen as satanic, but also pastoral and even Christ-like. He was both a goaty devil *and* a shepherd of his flocks. He was both animal and spiritual.

There were, of course, numerous deities from the pagan past that could have been revived. Egyptian gods such as Isis had some currency with Aleister Crowley and others; Dionysus and Bacchus also

---

22　See, for example, Robert Graves' poem of 1917, *To Robert Nichols*, in which he recognises that verses about 'sleek fauns,' drunk in the summer, are redundant in such times.

had some adherents;[23] but the latter was generally subsumed into the cult of his companion Pan, who stood for all the pagan gods. This probably derived from his universal character and from his adaptability, as just described.

---

23   See, for example, *Reveille* by Michael Field, or James Elroy Flecker, *The Bridge of Fire* or *The Ballad of Hampstead Heath*.

CHAPTER 4

Prayers to Pan

There was something of a crisis of confidence in Christianity during the mid-nineteenth century. This is most memorably expressed by Matthew Arnold (1822–88) in his poem *Dover Beach*, in which he described how:

> "The Sea of Faith
> Was once, too, at the full, and round earth's shore
> Lay like the folds of a bright girdle furled.
> But now I only hear
> Its melancholy, long, withdrawing roar,
> Retreating, to the breath
> Of the night-wind, down the vast edges drear
> And naked shingles of the world."

There were various responses to this sense of weakening belief. Some forsook the Church of England for Roman Catholicism; others began to seriously reconsider the religion of the Greeks and Romans that they had learned about at school. Whilst the pantheism of Wordsworth and Coleridge had been a sense of the divine suffused in nature, and was in many respects a new manner of expressing conventional sentiments, some of the newer thinking was more consciously 'pagan.' Even the Poet Laureate, Sir Alfred Tennyson, wrote a poem on *The Higher Pantheism,* although this was probably more of a fashionable gloss upon standard Christian belief than any genuine commitment to new gods – and as such was mocked pitilessly by Algernon Swinburne in his *The Higher Pantheism in a Nutshell.*

Some individuals seem to have been more sincere in their expressions of devotion to the ancient gods, for example Robert Williams Buchanan (1841–1901), who asked:

> "O who will worship the great god Pan
>   Out in the woods with me,
>   Now the chestnut spreadeth its seven-leaved fan
>   Over the hive of the bee?
>   Now the cushat cries, and the fallow deer
>   Creep on the woodland way,
>   O who will hearken, and try to hear
>   The voice of the god to-day?"

The challenge of this heterodoxy could not go ignored by the establishment. Several previous writers had repeated Plutarch's cry of "Pan is dead!" for dramatic effect,[24] but Elizabeth Barret Browning took it up with purpose, reacting to the challenge that Pan represented for the church. In her *Pan is Dead* she mocked the unresponsiveness of the classical gods – who were now debunked

---

24 See, for example, Blaise Pascal, *Pensées,* 'Prophecies' no.694; Theophile Gautier, 'Tombs and Funeral Pyres' in *Enamels and Cameos,* Madison Julius Cawein, *Thamus,* or Buchanan, 'Proteus, or a Prelude', stanza 3, in *The Undertones,* 1863.

and empty in her opinion. Neither the Olympian deities or the many lesser gods of the countryside had any validity, she felt – whether she was thinking of the anonymous nymphs or the great figures such as Apollo, Jove, Juno, Pallas, Bacchus, Hermes or the rest. She hammered home her message that they were as dead as their surviving marble statutes:

"Do ye leave your rivers flowing
　All alone, O Naiades,
While your drenchéd locks dry slow in
This cold feeble sun and breeze?
Not a word the Naiads say,
Though the rivers run for aye.
　　　For Pan is dead.

From the gloaming of the oak-wood,
O ye Dryads, could ye flee?
At the rushing thunderstroke would
No sob tremble through the tree?
Not a word the Dryads say,
Though the forests wave for aye.
　　　For Pan is dead.

Have ye left the mountain places,
Oreads wild, for other tryst?
Shall we see no sudden faces
Strike a glory through the mist?
Not a sound the silence thrills
Of the everlasting hills.
　　　Pan, Pan is dead."

For Browning, these gods had long ago been rendered impotent and irrelevant by the advent of the Christian saviour. In the face of the resurrected Jesus, the symbol of divine love, the Greek and Roman pantheon had been exposed and deposed as mere myth and fiction:

> "Gods bereavéd, gods belated,
>> With your purples rent asunder!
>> Gods discrowned and desecrated,
>> Disinherited of thunder!
>> Now, the goats may climb and crop
>> The soft grass on Ida's top—
>>> Now, Pan is dead."

In the face of truth, they had fled, their modern silence proof of their vacancy. They were dead and palsied, "dull and senseless," reduced to an "idiocy of godhead." Browning's tone is triumphant and scornful. French poet Guillaume Appollinaire likewise saw the birth of Jesus as the doom of the Olympians (*Pan est Mort*). By way of contrast, however, it is worth noting that G. K. Chesterton proposed quite an opposite effect: "When Jesus Christ was born, Pan began to stir in his grave." His reasoning was that by treating the pagan gods as devils, the early Christians' Church had given them life and validity again and had, unwittingly, "resurrected all the supernatural instincts of forests and hills."[25]

The Lost God by Francis Bourdillon (1891) played upon the same themes as Browning's poem. Two lovers, Leander and Helen, briefly break a sea voyage upon an island. As they explore, he describes to her his recent dream vision of the cremation of Pan,

---

25   Chesterton, *William Blake*, 1910, 107–8.

"The human god who loves the world of men... Earth's one link left with Heaven." They are both mystified by the vision – how a god could die. Leander, however, suggests that Pan being part-human, and always dwelling with men, perhaps could succumb to mortality. Helen then asks:

"How think you then? Did Pan love men so well
    That he put off his immortality
    To dwell among them? What dread Power is that,
    Inexorable, dealing thus the lots
    Of mortal and immortal? Is there God
    Above the gods? Could he not break his laws
    Being his own, and spare the one kind god,
    Albeit transgressing?"

This leads the lovers to further speculation. Leander recalls occasions when he was out in the natural world and felt a sense of holiness and euphoria – yet Pan was nowhere near him. "Long I thought/ Such ecstasies the effluence of Pan," he says, but now he wonders if in fact a higher deity still might have created the world. The couple know Pan is the inspirer of poetry, and are thankful for this, but they doubt that any god would relinquish his immortality for men. Leander resolves that, if the god to whom he had formerly dedicated himself and his poetry has truly died, he will move on and will travel the world in search of another meaning for his life. In so doing, he eventually meets a Greek called Philo who converts him to the new Christian religion. Leander then returns to Helen and they both accept the 'authentic' god who has chosen to manifest in human form, who put off his immortality out of a genuine love of humans. Jesus resembles Pan, and vice versa. Bourdillon saw the incarnation as a false god being exposed;

others, though, could turn that reasoning on its head and turn to Pan as an older manifestation of the same idea.

Elizabeth Barrett Browning's disparagement of false devotion notwithstanding, even as she asserted their redundancy, or rather their falseness, the poet could not, at the same time, resist the allure of the myths. In *A Musical Instrument*, she rehearsed the story of Pan and Syrinx, asking:

> "What was he doing, the great god Pan,
>   Down in the reeds by the river?
>   Spreading ruin and scattering ban,
>   Splashing and paddling with hoofs of a goat,
>   And breaking the golden lilies afloat
>   With the dragon-fly on the river."

He may be brute and violent, yet in cutting reeds to craft pipes, he is the originator of poetry and sweet music. Browning plainly felt torn between the power of the story's symbolism and an aversion to the power of pagan imagery. She concluded with words that recognised Pan's role in inspiration, but which at the same time rejected his validity:

> "Yet half a beast is the great god Pan,
>   To laugh as he sits by the river,
>   Making a poet out of a man:
>   The true gods sigh for the cost and pain—
>   For the reed which grows nevermore again
>   As a reed with the reeds in the river."

Browning's husband, Robert, seemed to share his wife's equivocal attitude to the ancient gods. His poem *Pan and Luna* describes the goat god's entrapment and seduction of the Moon. He seems very prepared to suspend disbelief:

> "Oh, worthy of belief I hold it was,
> Virgil, your legend in those strange three lines!
> No question, that adventure came to pass
> One black night in Arcadia:"

What's more, Browning's description of Luna's naked form gets quite overheated; he was evidently able to sense another, vital power within those myths. The orthodox assertions of the demise of Pan were often tinged with regret, therefore; there was a sense that with his absence, something had been lost. Lady Margaret Sackville (1881–1963) was just one to have expressed that ambivalence:

> "Those perverse pipes which lure men's feet to stray
> From the ancient safety of the straight highway,
> To worship on some perilous hillside
> That loveliness which perished when Pan died."[26]

The cult had its defects, but it had engendered thoughts of beauty, joy, life and, for some, liberated, unbridled passion.

The raw – and very possibly alarming – nature of the passions that the ancient god could evoke comes through in one of the poems of Aleister Crowley. *Dionysus* is a hymn to that god, as well as to his companion, in which Crowley celebrates "the festal mystical revel/ The rapturous Bacchanal rite." Moreover, he promises that:

---

26   Sackville, *Prelude*.

"Ye shall see things as they are!
  I lift the mask of matter;
  I open the heart of man;
  For I am of force to shatter
  The cast that hideth – Pan!
  Your loves shall lap up slaughter,
  And dabbled with roses of blood
  Each desperate darling daughter
  Shall swim in the fervid flood.
  I bring ye laughter and tears,
  The kisses that foam and bleed,
  The joys of a million years…"

The gods' worshippers are assured that they shall experience something transcendental and transforming:

"Ye shall pass in pleasure and peril
  Across the mystical bar
  That is set for wrath and weeping
  Against the children of earth;
  But ye in singing and sleeping
  Shall pass in measure and mirth!

In conclusion, Crowley cries out in ecstasy: "We are wed, we are wild, we are one!" For the Order of the Golden Dawn, Pan symbolised the raw generative powers of nature – yet was not a particular focus of their reverence. When Crowley split from the Order and established the *Argenteum Astrum*, Pan assumed greater significance in their rites: he was the deity of lust and magic; the spirit of the infinite all and the hope of all humanity. This vision is encapsulated in the poetry of Victor Neuburg,

Crowley's collaborator. In his collection, *The Triumph of Pan,* he exclaims, variously:

"Now I am free from the sod;
　Priapus hath grown into Pan."

"One in Pan are we!"

"There shall be no despair,
　But Pan! Pan! Pan! And all the world shall be
　Mingled in one wild burning ecstasy."

"... oh, scan,
　The vision of great Pan.
　Thrust tongue and limbs against his side
　And thou shalt know the dayspring as a bride!"

"I seek the hidden grove
　Where Pan plays to the trees
　The nymphs, the fauns, the breeze..."[27]

Such ecstatic utterances, audible proof of the stirring of powerful, elemental forces, represented a severe existential challenge to the staid and sober Christian. In *Pan Worship,* of 1908, Eleanor Farjeon recognised the apparent decay of the ancient faith in the face of nearly two thousand years of Christian ascendancy, but was not discouraged:

27　Neuburg, *The Triumph of Pan,* 1910, 'The Romance of Olivia Vane' &
　　'The Triumph of Pan.'

"In Arcady there lies a crystal spring
    Ring'd all about with green melodious reeds
    Swaying seal'd music up and down the wind.
    Here on its time-defacèd pedestal
    The image of a half-forgotten God
    Crumbles to its complete oblivion."

The ancient temples, "Pan's lost dominion," may be overgrown
and neglected, but they are still evocative:

"All my breast aches with longing for the past!
    Thou God of stone, I have a craving in me
    For knowledge of thee as thou wert in old
    Enchanted twilights in Arcadia."

She calls on the god to come again with all his mythical companions
for:

"The pagan in my blood, the instinct in me
    That yearns back, back to nature-worship, cries
    Aloud to thee!"

Farjeon is ready to offer milk and honey in sacrifice and to play a
reed pipe to invoke his name:

"O Pan, old Pan,
    Shall I not see thee stirring in the stone,
    Crack thy confinement, leap forth—be again?
    I can believe it, master of bright streams,
    Lord of green woodlands, king of sun-spread plains
    And star-splashed hills and valleys drenched in moonlight!

And I shall see again a dance of Dryads
And airy shapes of Oreads circling free
To shy sweet pipings of fantastic fauns
And lustier-breathing satyrs ... God of Nature,
Thrice hailing thee by name with boisterous lungs
I will thrill thee back from the dead ages, thus:
Pan! Pan! O Pan! bring back thy reign again
Upon the earth!"

Christian culture insisted upon the defeat of pagan fantasies and the disappearance of the mythical beings, who had been reduced to daydreams and mere stories. Irish poet William Allingham referred to Pan in the same sentence as Oberon, reducing both to fairy tale figures, fit only for nurseries.[28] Not all poets were ready to concede that the Olympian gods had been utterly banished, though, and given that the Church was still fulminating against the Greek gods two millennia after their purported defeat, perhaps they were right. In his poem *Panthea,* Oscar Wilde reflected Allingham's approach by grouping together those creatures of myth, the fauns, centaurs and elves; nonetheless, in *Santa Decca* he expressed a sense of hopeful ambivalence:

"The Gods are dead: no longer do we bring
To grey-eyed Pallas crowns of olive-leaves!
Demeter's child no more hath tithe of sheaves,
And in the noon the careless shepherds sing,
For Pan is dead, and all the wantoning
By secret glade and devious haunt is o'er:

---

28   For instance, Bulwer-Lytton, 'The Complaint of the Last Faun' and 'The Ideal World' in *Pilgrim of the Rhine,* 1865; William Allingham, *The Daffodil.*

47

Young Hylas seeks the water-springs no more;
Great Pan is dead, and Mary's son is King.

And yet – perchance in this sea-trancèd isle,
Chewing the bitter fruit of memory,
Some God lies hidden in the asphodel.
Ah Love! if such there be, then it were well
For us to fly his anger: nay, but see,
The leaves are stirring: let us watch awhile."

Robert Louis Stevenson made one of the most compelling cases for the continued relevance of the god in 'Pan's Pipes,' chapter eleven of *Virginibus Puerisque* (1897). He appreciated that Pan was gaining new relevance for the young and the curious and that, like all natural forces, he could not be denied:

> "The world in which we live has been variously said and sung by the most ingenious poets and philosophers: these reducing it to formulæ and chemical ingredients, those striking the lyre in high-sounding measures for the handiwork of God. What experience supplies is of a mingled tissue, and the choosing mind has much to reject before it can get together the materials of a theory...
>
> The Greeks figured Pan, the God of Nature, now terribly stamping his foot, so that armies were dispersed; now by the woodside on a summer noon trilling on his pipe until he charmed the hearts of upland ploughmen. And the Greeks, in so figuring, uttered the last word of human experience. To certain smoke-dried spirits matter and motion and elastic aethers, and the hypothesis of this or that other spectacled professor, tell a speaking story;

but for youth and all ductile and congenial minds, Pan is
not dead, but of all the classic hierarchy alone survives in
triumph; goat-footed, with a gleeful and an angry look, the
type of the shaggy world: and in every wood, if you go
with a spirit properly prepared, you shall hear the note of
his pipe.

[Rivers and birdsong and rain] are all airs upon Pan's
pipe; he it was who gave them breath in the exultation of
his heart, and gleefully modulated their outflow with his
lips and fingers... it puts a spirit of gladness in all hearts;
and to look on the happy side of nature is common, in their
hours, to all created things... [Different people respond to
this in different ways] But let him feign never so carefully,
there is not a man but has his pulses shaken when Pan
trolls out a stave of ecstasy and sets the world a-singing.

Alas if that were all! But oftentimes the air is changed;
and in the screech of the night wind, chasing navies,
subverting the tall ships and the rooted cedar of the hills;
in the random deadly levin or the fury of headlong floods,
we recognise the "dread foundation" of life and the anger
in Pan's heart... [Life is loss as well as joy.] Earth wages
open war against her children, and under her softest touch
hides treacherous claws... The cool waters invite us in
to drown; the domestic hearth burns up in the hour of
sleep, and makes an end of all. Everything is good or bad,
helpful or deadly, not in itself, but by its circumstances...
For death is given in a kiss; the dearest kindnesses are
fatal; and into this life, where one thing preys upon
another, the child too often makes its entrance from the
mother's corpse. It is no wonder, with so traitorous a
scheme of things, if the wise people who created for us the

idea of Pan thought that of all fears the fear of him was the most terrible, since it embraces all. And still we preserve the phrase: a panic terror. To reckon dangers too curiously, to hearken too intently for the threat that runs through all the winning music of the world, to hold back the hand from the rose because of the thorn, and from life because of death: this it is to be afraid of Pan. Highly respectable citizens who flee life's pleasures and responsibilities and keep, with upright hat, upon the midway of custom, avoiding the right hand and the left, the ecstasies and the agonies, how surprised they would be if they could hear their attitude mythologically expressed, and knew themselves as tooth-chattering ones, who flee from Nature because they fear the hand of Nature's God! Shrilly sound Pan's pipes; and behold the banker instantly concealed in the bank parlour! For to distrust one's impulses is to be recreant [cowardly or unfaithful] to Pan.

[Beyond science there is joy and uncertainty – which can only be satisfied by art.] So we come back to the old myth, and hear the goat-footed piper making the music which is itself the charm and terror of things; and when a glen invites our visiting footsteps, fancy that Pan leads us thither with a gracious tremolo; or when our hearts quail at the thunder of the cataract, tell ourselves that he has stamped his hoof in the nigh thicket."

The continuing struggle of the church and the classical gods was dramatised thirty years later in Lord Dunsany's 1928 novel *The Blessing of Pan*. The ongoing conflict between Christianity and paganism is given vivid reality when the entire population of the isolated English village of Wolding is seduced away from the Christian Church by the hypnotic piping of a seventeen-year-old, Tommy Duffin. The book is much more a satire upon the ineffectiveness, complacency and self-absorption of an Anglican Church too interested in trivial worldly affairs than it is a paean to the cult of Pan, but the story is told through the eyes of the local parson, the Reverend Elderick Anwrel. His struggle against heresy in his remote parish is met with indifference and a lack of realism by the Church hierarchy. His bishop suggests that getting the village boys interested in cricket might distract them from the lure of the pagan rites.

It is very hard for the parson to compete with the ancient deity. Duffin acts as Pan's herald, sneaking out at night to play his reed pipes at some local megaliths – the Old Stones of Wolding. His music is irresistible, stirring up thoughts of an older way of living – less material, less concerned with manufacturing and consumption. Firstly, the village girls succumb, then the young men, and then almost everybody else (including Anwrel's wife) joins in the dancing to Duffin's haunting and compelling tunes on top of Wold Hill.

The problem (if you want to view it this way) with the renewed worship of Pan is that the local people start to neglect their daily chores. A farmer leaves his hay in the field; the postman doesn't deliver the letters and Anwrel's maid doesn't do the cleaning. Instead, at the village school, the children are taught the phrase *"ego Pan panton ton lophon Arkadiou basileus"* (I, Pan, the king of all the Arcadian slopes).

Pan offers the villagers joyful liberation, something the Church of England can't provide. Anwrel realises that his flock have lost faith in one set of beliefs and have chosen, or rather re-discovered, another. They've substituted one 'illusion' for another but, as one of the characters remarks, "Pan was always friendly to Man... We may have changed a lot this last two thousand years; but that's you and me still. Why, I'd let him come nosing in."

The parson finally tries to preach against paganism in a Sunday sermon, appealing rather weakly to this parishioners' sense of community faith, the beliefs of their forebears, but he realises he is up against a much older faith that is embedded in the very land of England. Tommy Duffin appears again with his pipes and slowly the entire congregation slips away, leaving the parson alone. That night, even Anwrel succumbs to the lure of the pipes, and sacrifices a bull with a Palaeolithic flint axe. He is re-united with his community and the people of Wolding, content in their recovery of the "old ways," settle into their quiet retreat from modernity, becoming increasingly self-sufficient and isolated, happy in their reconnection with nature, the land and the seasons. They give up cultivation and return to the local woods for their food, allowing weeds to take over the fields. Nature and paganism win out in *The Blessing of Pan;* belonging proves to be more important than orthodoxy.

There was an energy and sense of liberty in the worship of Pan which the established churches simply could not offer. Pan recognised the realities of Nature – of human nature and of the natural world. Pan offered excitement, daring and an opportunity for complete self-expression against the allure of which centuries of Christianity, with its burden of sin and guilt, its Puritan austerity and its rejection and horror of the flesh, struggled to compete. Matthew Arnold had found himself on a "darkling plain/ Swept with confused alarms of struggle and fight." Pan offered an alternative to this. With the right perspective and perception, individuals could discover that the hills (and, for that matter, the woods) were alive with the sound of piping. Pan had already lasted for thousands of years and there was still no reason to regard him as inert or irrelevant:

> "... But I had seen
> That Pan still lives and all his train,
> Whatever men say: they remain
> The unseen forces; they that mean
> Nature; its awe and majesty,
> That symbolise mythology."[29]

---

29   Madison Julius Cawein, *Wood Myths*.

CHAPTER 5

In Praise
of Pan

"Pan's a King, and shepherds are his subjects!"[30]

We turn now to examine the multiple visions of Pan that existed during the mid-nineteenth century and afterwards. Perceptions of the god developed upon the same foundations of an education in the classics at public and grammar schools that were mentioned earlier when discussing the Renaissance. The ancient Greek and Roman texts continued to provide a context and a touchstone for the thinking of new generations. The myths of gods and heroes gave them a rich treasury of plots, characters, incidents and quotations to which they resorted almost by instinct. Many of these stories were better known to them than their own native legends; it is little surprise that they preferred them out of habit. It was no conscious archaising then, for Irish poet and novelist James

---

30 Aleister Crowley, *Apollo in Pherae.*

Stephens (1880–1950) to compose a poem called *The Centaurs*.[31]

Pan is the god of grazing lands, groves – and girls. He is a simple, straightforward and innocent god, in many ways.[32] He is a deity of the natural world, an expression and celebration of uninhibited natural processes; he is found near at hand for our worship in flowers and foliage. He is ever present and latent around us in the natural world – easy to contact and easy to love. Different facets of his personality and cult were identified by writers and brought to the fore in their works.

FOREST KING

At his most circumscribed, Pan could be envisaged as a sylvan deity. His was the brown face seen briefly amongst the summer leaves; his was the running form that flitted between the tree trunks. He was the soul of the woods and wild places who might sometimes be glimpsed or, even, stumbled upon.[33]

For Elenore Farjeon, Pan was the "God of Nature,""Lord of green woodlands" (as well as of being "King of sun-spread plains/ And star-splashed hills and valleys drenched in moonlight!"). His deep domain was the wildwood, he was "immortal [and]

---

31 The US poet Madison Julius Cawein, who will be much quoted here, also made fulsome use of classical imagery in his poetry: see for example *Myth & Romance, The Limnad, Wood Myths, Dreamer of Dreams, Forest & Field, Dionysia, In Mythic Seas, Loveliness, Late October, Transformation, Artemis, Dionysos* or *Dithyrambics*.

32 Henry Nevinson, *The Plea of Pan*, 1901; see too 'In Thessaly,' Arthur Davidson Ficke, *From the Isles*, 1907, in which Pan is deity of the dispossessed.

33 See, for example, Madison Cawein, *Forest of Old Enchantment*, 1913; *Moss & Fern, Genius Loci* and *Wood God*.

wood-pervading, "the "genius of the wood."[34] The trees can sing his praises – and, in fact, the reverence and joy is mutual:

> "Us
> The joy of the wild woods never
> Leaves free of the thirst it slakes:
> The wild love throbs in us ever
> That burns in the dense hot brakes
> Thus."[35]

Pan seems to appear as the mysterious 'King of the Wood' in the story titled 'The Fairy Wife' in Maurice Hewlett's *Lore of Proserpine*, 1913. In fact, Hewlett had already tackled the same plot in his *Pan and the Young Shepherd: A Pastoral in Two Acts* of 1899. This earlier composition concerned a shepherd boy, Neanias, who becomes dissatisfied with his lot watching the flocks and wants to see the world and find adventure. What he does manage to do is to go into a deep forest and meet the Seven Sisters (world spirits) who all love and woo him. He chooses the least bold of them, Aglae (or Virgin Dawn), who cannot speak. He carries her back to his home where all love her except Marla, who was Neanias' childhood sweetheart. Out of jealousy, Marla encourages Pan to carry Aglae off – but she is retrieved by her lover and gains the power of speech.

Hewlett's later handling of the story, titled the 'Fairy Wife,' is virtually identical, although all the names are changed and events are transferred to a remote Borders village deep in the Cheviot Hills. Now it is sheep farmer Andrew King who is drawn into the haunted forest of Knapp where stand the group of trees called the Seven

---

34 Farjeon, *Pan Worship;* Robert Browning, *Pan & Luna;* Buchanan, *Pan;* Cawein, *Wood God.*

35 Swinburne, *Pan & Thalassius.*

Sisters. He had been there before, and had been seized with sudden freezing fear (panic, or the Stroke of Pan), but he couldn't resist the urge to visit again. This time he discovers six young women dancing – evidently wood-nymphs. They see him and swarm upon him, each trying to seduce him, but he chooses the seventh, silent sister, whom he finds cowering nearby at the foot of a beech tree. The couple marry but, once again, the girl is taken back by The Master, the King of the Wood, during a terrible spring storm. She is recovered by Andrew and gains her voice, whilst it is reported that one of the Seven Sister trees had been felled by the wind.[36]

There was a risk, however, that the perception of Pan as a solely woodland god could become limiting or debasing, that the god's function could be linked to other nature spirits and thereby diminished. This was not mere theory; there was a genuine danger of it happening. For example, US poet Joyce Kilmer (1886–1918) equated Pan with much more harmless sprites whom, he proposed, were only revealed to the innocent simplicity of youth:

> "[He] sees with eyes by ignorance made keen
> The fauns and elves whom older eyes disperse,
> Great Pan and all the fairies with their queen."

Another American poet, Madison Julius Cawein, also combined classical and British tradition, conjuring up a "Wood of Dreams,/ Where, as of old, dwell Fay and Faun,/And Faërie dances until dawn."[37]

---

36 The classical Seven Sisters, the Pleiades, are nymphs, daughters of the titan Atlas and the sea nymph Pleione. They are half-sisters to the nymphs Calypso, the Hyades and the Hesperides. They have no especial connection with trees, though.

37 Kilmer, *For a Child*, 1918; Cawein, *Wood Dreams*, 1913.

The fairies and elves of British tradition had already been reduced, both physically and spiritually, and associating Pan too closely with a mythology that was already weakened and trivialised posed exactly the same risks to his cult.

HYMNS TO LIFE

Beyond this tendency towards cosiness, though, one of Pan's most fundamental aspects remained his symbolisation of the processes of growth and renewal. More broadly, he represents the superiority or authenticity of the natural creation as against the man-made world. As Walter Besant and James Rice expressed very well in their fairy story, *Titania's Farewell*, published in 1878:

> "The old nature worship goes on as ever. Great God Pan never dies."[38]

A very simple expression of these sentiments is Algernon Swinburne's poem, *The Palace of Pan*, which was written in September 1893. He describes a forest, which he treats as a temple to the god. Within the depths of the trees, "mute worship... possesses the spirit with peace." The poet feels that he's near to the god's mystery and that he will soon encounter "Some track of a nymph's or some trail of a faun's/ To the place of the slumber of Pan." He finds himself seized "with passionate awe that is deeper than panic" and experiences the sensation of:

---

38   Besant & Rice, *The Case of Mr Lucraft & Other Stories*, 1878.

"The spirit made one with the spirit whose breath,
Makes noon in the woodland sublime."

A prose counterpart of Swinburne's poem might be the Algernon Blackwood short story, *The Man Who Played Upon a Leaf*.[39] The narrator of the story is taking a holiday in a small village in the Swiss Jura when he encounters a vagabond man and his faithful dog. The man plays music on nothing more than an ivy leaf held between his hands, but is able to produce the sounds of nature – the wind, bird song and trees stirring. His music is arresting, transporting and, one man complains, it causes strange dreams. The visitor and the beggar strike up a friendship, because the musician can see that the tourist understands in his soul what the music means. The beggar plays for "the God of the Forests." He is a "self-appointed Priest of Pan" or an "unwitting votary of Pan." The Englishman gives him food and coins, but he does not keep them for himself. Instead, he offers them to "the god" at a spot that is his 'Holy of Holies' in the forest – a natural hollow filled with lilies where the trees look like the columns of a cathedral. It is secluded, peaceful and a natural shrine which inspired enchantment and reverence – just as Swinburne described and just as the character Leander in Bourdillon's *Lost God* had experienced.

Watching a full moon in an August sky, American poet Emma Lazarus found, like Swinburne, Bourdillon and Brooke, that the beauty of nature conjured up for her thoughts of mythical beings – sylphs, nymphs, undines, fauns, mermaids, elves, the summer fairies – Mab and Ariel and Puck – and "Universal Pan." However, she felt these were all "classic types outworn" that could not stand

---

39   From *The Lost Valley and Other Stories*, 1910.

in the way of the progress of truth and beauty, art and science combined.[40]

This, then, was the practical new religion that could replace both Christ and Pan – an understanding of creation through science. Yet it seemed sterile to many of Lazarus' contemporaries. Only six years later Edmund Clarence Stedman wrote *Pan in Wall Street*, deliberately challenging so materialist a view of the way forward. Just outside the Treasury building in Wall Street, he hears strange, wild music and has a vision of ancient priests and Pan himself, "A-strolling through this sordid city,/ And piping to the civic ear/ The prelude of some pastoral ditty!" He was dressed in a cap and shoes, but his horns and hooves were unmistakeable. His pipe music drew, inescapably, all the stock exchange traders and other New York city dwellers. The busy scene is transformed and the poet dares to hope:

"O heart of Nature, beating still
  With throbs her vernal passion taught her,
  Even here as on the vine-clad hill
  Or by the Arethusan water!
  New forms may fold the speech, new lands
  Arise within these ocean portals,
  But music waves eternal wands,
  Enchantress of the souls of mortals!"

That is, until a policeman moves the vagrant piper along and the spell is broken.[41]

---

40 Lazarus, *Autumn Moon*, 1861.
41 Stedman, *Pan on Wall Street*, 1867.

Stedman deliberately deflated his pastoral lyricism in his final stanza, but many other poets had greater faith in the power of Pan. Edna St Vincent Millay dared to believe that the god's power was renewed every spring with the rebirth of nature:

> "Doubt no more that Oberon—
> Never doubt that Pan
> Lived, and played a reed, and ran
> After nymphs in a dark forest,
> In the merry, credulous days—
> Lived, and led a fairy band
> Over the indulgent land!
> Ah, for in this dourest, sorest
> Age man's eye has looked upon,
> Death to fauns and death to fays,
> Still the dog-wood dares to raise—
> Healthy tree, with trunk and root—
> Ivory bowls that bear no fruit,
> And the starlings and the jays—
> Birds that cannot even sing—
> Dare to come again in spring!"[42]

Exactly the same was true of Walter De La Mare:

> "They told me Pan was dead, but I
> Oft marvelled who it was that sang
> Down the green valleys languidly
> Where the grey elder-thickets hang.

---

42 Edna St Vincent Millay, *Doubt No More*, 1921.

Sometimes I thought it was a bird
My soul had charged with sorcery;
Sometimes it seemed my own heart heard
Inland the sorrow of the sea.

But even where the primrose sets
The seal of her pale loveliness,
I found amid the violets
Tears of an antique bitterness."[43]

Pan was at the heart of regrowth and renewal:

"… in my veins a new and natural youth,
In my great veins a music as of boughs
When the cool aspen-fingers of the Rain
Feel for the eyelids of the earth in spring,
In every vein quick life…"[44]

He was all the bounty and beauty of nature:

"God Pan, from the glad wood's portal
The breaths of thy song blow sweet:
Thine
All secrets of growth and of birth are,
All glories of flower and of tree,
Wheresoever the wonders of earth are;"[45]

---

43 De la Mare, *They Told Me*, 1906.
44 Robert Buchanan, *Pan*.
45 Swinburne, *Pan & Thalassius*.

Pan, as God of Nature, could not in fact die because he was annually reborn and renewed. Walter Henley celebrated this exuberantly in his poem, *Allegro Maestoso*:

> "Praise God for giving
>> Through this His messenger among the days
>> His word the life He gave is thrice-worth living!
>> For Pan, the bountiful, imperious Pan—
>> Not dead, not dead, as impotent dreamers feigned,
>> But the gay genius of a million Mays
>> Renewing his beneficent endeavour!—
>> Still reigns and triumphs, as he hath triumphed and reigned
>> Since in the dim blue dawn of time
>> The universal ebb-and-flow began,
>> To sound his ancient music, and prevails..."[46]

But, as Swinburne appreciated, whilst Pan is lord of all "green world's pleasance," he is also something fierce and wild:

> "The joy of the wild woods never
>> Leaves free of the thirst it slakes:
>> The wild love throbs in us ever
>> That burns in the dense hot brakes
>> Thus.
>> Life,
>> Eternal, passionate, awless,
>> Insatiable, mutable, dear,
>> Makes all men's law for us lawless:
>> We strive not: how should we fear

---

46   See similar panegyrics in Bliss Carman, *Pan in the Catskills* or James Elroy Flecker, *Oak & Olive*.

Strife?
We,
The birds and the bright winds know not
Such joys as are ours in the mild
Warm woodland..."

Of course, Swinburne was suspect to many during his life for the very reason that he expressed the intensity with which wild love could throb. Literary critic John Morley attacked the writer's *Poems and Ballads* of 1866 for their "feverish carnality" and "nameless shameless abominations," Swinburne himself being condemned as "the libidinous laureate of a pack of satyrs."[47]

Such natural exuberant power as Swinburne expressed is always balanced on the edge of something less benign and more uncontrolled.[48] One manifestation of this is in Pan's sexual appetites where, as we shall discover, his passion for nymphs can sometimes become too urgent and too forceful. Lady Margaret Sackville captured this divine duality in a poem on the nymph *Syrinx*. She recognises that there is "something bestial and divine" present in the god – both at the same time – and that he functions simultaneously as:

"lord of death and birth,
    And the year wanes and waxes as he wills.
    Yea, very spirit is he and heart of earth.
    And cruel as untempered rain and sun,
    In those sick seasons when all falls to dearth.
    And there shall none resist him, nay not one..."

---

47 Morley, *Saturday Review,* 1866.
48 See, for example artist Stephen McKenna's 1926 novel, *The Oldest God.*

The natural world can be undiscriminating and harsh just as easily as it can be mild and lovely. We shall return later to some of the more damaging or dangerous aspects of Pan's personality, but we should also recognise that this aspect might manifest rather as a divine power that provokes awe. Despite the pessimism that we just saw him express, at the heart of Kenneth Grahame's *Wind in the Willows* is the chapter *The Piper at the Gates of Dawn*. This contains some of the most lyrical passages in the book, as it describes the mystical encounter between Mole, Ratty and Pan.

The two river creatures are out in a boat at night, searching for a lost baby otter. Just as the sky begins to brighten, they hear music: "beautiful and strange and new... it has roused a longing... that is pain, and nothing seems worthwhile but just to hear that sound once more and go on listening to it forever." The water rat hears it first, and is possessed and transported by the "merry bubble and joy, the thin, clear, happy call of the distant piping! Such music I never dreamed of, and the call in it is stronger even than the music is sweet! Row on, Mole, row! For the music and the call must be for us." They land at a hidden island and find a clearing amidst wild fruit trees. A deep silence falls and:

> "Then suddenly the Mole felt a great Awe fall upon him,
> an awe that turned his muscles to water, bowed his head,
> and rooted his feet to the ground. It was no panic terror –
> indeed he felt wonderfully at peace and happy – but it was
> an awe that smote and held him and, without seeing, he
> knew it could only mean that some august Presence was
> very, very near."

The pair struggle to look up to see the august presence before them. It was:

"the Friend and Helper; [they] saw the backward sweep
of the curved horns, gleaming in the growing daylight;
saw the stern, hooked nose between the kindly eyes
that were looking down on them humorously, while the
bearded mouth broke into a half-smile at the corners; saw
the rippling muscles on the arm that lay across the broad
chest, the long supple hand still holding the pan-pipes only
just fallen away from the parted lips; saw the splendid
curves of the shaggy limbs disposed in majestic ease on
the sward..."

The two small creatures are overwhelmed with unutterable love
and the pair bow down and worship him. Then the sun rises fully
and the vision vanishes – leaving only the baby otter, curled up
and asleep. In turn, a sense of great loss and dumb misery engulfs
them both, until at that moment a little breeze arose:

"and blew lightly and caressingly in their faces; and with its
soft touch came instant oblivion. For this is the last best
gift that the kindly demi-god is careful to bestow on those
to whom he has revealed himself in their helping: the
gift of forgetfulness. Lest the awful remembrance should
remain and grow, and overshadow mirth and pleasure, and
the great haunting memory should spoil all the after-lives
of little animals helped out of difficulties, in order that
they should be happy and light-hearted as before."

Instantly, they struggle to recall what had gone just before, as
if they had awoken from a beautiful dream and it was melting
quickly away. Some hoof marks in the earth puzzle Ratty for a
moment, but the time has come to take the lost otter child home.

These beautiful paragraphs evoke for us Pan the protector, the friend and saviour of wild animals – a far more benign and kindly vision than most we shall find.[49]

PAN AND THE ENVIRONMENT

Worship of Pan, therefore, could be expressed through communion with nature and – it was argued by some – this was the primary expression of the cult in the late nineteenth century (even, perhaps, though it was done almost unwittingly). English author Richard Le Galliene (1866–1947) explored this in his 1915 collection of essays, *Vanishing Roads*. He proposed that an attraction to the countryside "is one of those encouraging signs of the times, which links one with the great brotherhood of men and women that have heard the call of the great god Pan, as he sits by the river." Increasingly, he felt, people were being united by the allure of the natural world – whether for sporting or aesthetic or spiritual reasons – and:

> "That combination of results can only come by the
> satisfaction of the undeniable religious instinct in all of
> us: an instinct that seeks goodness, but seeks happiness
> too. Now, there are creeds by which you can be good
> without being happy; and creeds by which you can be
> happy without being good. But, perhaps, there is only one
> creed by which you can be both at once – the creed of the
> growing grass, and the blue sky and the running river, the
> creed of the dog-wood and the skunk-cabbage, the creed

---

49   Grahame, *The Wind in the Willows*, 1908, c.7.

of the red-wing and the blue heron – the creed of the great
god Pan."

This often unspoken and unexpressed yearning for the outdoors
was a clear indication that the reports of Pan's death had been
premature, because:

> "Pan, of course, could only die with the earth itself, and
> so long as the lichen and the moss keep quietly at their
> work on the grey boulder, and the lightning zigzags down
> through the hemlocks, and the arrowhead guards its waxen
> blossom in the streams; so long as the earth shakes with
> the thunder of hoofs, or pours out its heart in the song of
> the veery-thrush, or bares its bosom in the wild rose, so
> long will there be little chapels to Pan in the woodland –
> chapels on the lintels of which you shall read, as Virgil
> wrote: Happy is he who knows the rural gods, Pan, and
> old Sylvanus, and the sister nymphs."

Le Galliene regarded this almost instinctual reverence for "the
green earth and the blue sea" as a manifestation of 'The Call of the
Wild.' It was not mere affectation or hobbyism, though. Rather, it
confirmed:

> "that the salvation of man is to be found on, and by means
> of, the green earth out of which he was born, and that, as
> there is no ill of his body which may not be healed by the
> magic juices of herb and flower, or the stern potency of
> minerals, so there is no sickness of his soul that may not
> be cured by the sound of the sea, the rustle of leaves, or
> the songs of birds.

Thirty or forty years ago the soul of the world was very sick. It had lost religion in a night of misunderstood 'materialism,' so-called. But since then that mere 'matter' which seemed to eclipse the soul has grown strangely radiant to deep-seeing eyes, and, whereas then one had to doubt everything, dupes of superficial disillusionment, now there is no old dream that has not the look of coming true, no hope too wild and strange and beautiful to be confidently entertained. Even if you wish to believe in fairies, science will hardly say you nay. Those dryads and fauns, which Keats saw 'frightened away' by the prosaic times in which it was his misfortune to be alive and unrecognized, are trooping back in every woodland..."

Pan was more than ever present – and praised – and his presence heals and reassures the world.[50]

Le Galliene was not, therefore, pessimistic. He might even be conceived of as an early environmentalist. Certainly, he felt confidence that, if sufficient numbers of people were respectful of the goat god, the future of the natural world need no longer be a cause for concern.

Others, such as Kenneth Grahame (who has been described as something of a 'weekend pagan'), were far less certain about the future for our environment, and fretted that the unspoiled world was under constant and worsening siege and attrition. Grahame was concerned that what looked to Le Galliene like a new style of living was only a brief respite from ever-accelerating destruction:

---

50   Le Galliene, *Vanishing Roads*, 1915, c.12 'The Spirit of the Open.'

"Happily, a great part is still spared… in which the rural
Pan and his following may hide their heads for yet a little
longer, until the growing tyranny has invaded the last
common, spinney, and sheep-down, and driven the kindly
god, the well-wisher to man – whither?"[51]

The perspective of another century or so may well incline us
to side with Grahame, but the point remains valid: that respect
and reverence for Pan in nature could be manifested practically
through its preservation.

NATURIST PAN

It seems obvious and instinctively right to honour Pan through
nudity outside. From this perception followed one of the most
basic expressions of the new interest in the natural world and a life
lived in closer contact with it: the late Victorian and Edwardian
enthusiasm for an outdoor lifestyle. Naked swimming, camping
and a vegetarian diet were all popular. Rupert Brooke, for
example, experienced one Easter holiday in Cornwall as a visit to
Arcady. He was discovered by a local woman dancing in a wood,
behaviour he tried to explain to her by declaring that Jesus was
dead but that Pan had risen with the Spring.[52]

It was not very far from this wish to seek recreational harmony
with nature to a more conscious wish to be at one with it. There has,
in fact, long been an interface between naturism and paganism. In
Britain, a leading proponent of nudism, paganism, vegetarianism

---

51   Kenneth Grahame, *Pagan Papers*, 'The Rural Pan – An April Essay.'
52   *Letters of Rupert Brooke*, 164.

and gay rights was the radical socialist pioneer, Edward Carpenter. Nudism had emerged as an ideal in the Romantic Movement, within which it was promoted as an authentic aspect of ancient Greek culture. Carpenter was inspired by this thinking, as well as finding an inherent romance in the liberation he felt the practice offered.

The German naturist movement, usually known by the name of *Freikörperkultur* (FKK), was the first such organisation in modern times and helped to establish nudity as a respectable lifestyle. The first FKK club was established in 1898 as part of a wider programme of so-called *Lebensreform*. This was a German social and cultural movement of the late-nineteenth and early-twentieth centuries that promulgated a back-to-nature philosophy. This favoured organic farming, vegetarianism, nudism, alternative therapies, anti-capitalism, and neo-paganism. Although it was politically diverse, a significant driving force came from the extreme right, through the so-called *Völkisch* movement which promoted a romantic German nationalism, combined with revived Teutonic pagan beliefs and (increasingly) racist ideas. More conservative Germans viewed the FKK as a symbol of moral decay, rather than as an expression of health and freedom, and when the Nazis came to power in 1933, nudist organisations were either banned or taken over. Even so, naturism was a difficult area for the National Socialists: some saw it as a way of developing a healthy Aryan folk; others feared that it led to immorality and homosexuality.

Quite separately from this, the emerging witchcraft movement in Britain promoted the idea of nudity as a natural and authentic state and the practice of working 'sky-clad' as an important – and powerful – symbolic gesture. It was seen as a liberating act that asserts the beauty of the body and brings the practitioner nearer to universal nature.

URBAN PAN

"One morning late in March, at the end of a long hard
winter, I was wakened by a flood of sunshine. The early
air came warm and soft through the open window; the first
magic suggestion of spring was abroad, with its whispered
hints of daffodils and budding hawthorns; and one's blood
danced to imagined pipings of Pan from happy fields far
distant..."[53]

It's understandable – automatic, even – to equate Pan with the
countryside and to assume that he has no place in urban areas.
Such a perception is reinforced by the feeling that Pan must
be perpetually opposed to progress and industry. In this vein,
Canadian poet Robert Frost contrasted the Pan of the untouched
wilderness to the encroachments of the modern world, and feared
that the god might have lost his place and his relevance: "They
were pipes of pagan mirth,/ And the world had found new terms
of worth." Both science and rational, factual prose seemed to have
eliminated the need and the space for Pan and his poetry.[54]

This antipathy need not necessarily be so. Matthew Arnold,
for example, found hints of Pan's presence, and snatches of his
refrains, even in Kensington Gardens in the heart of London
(where, of course, J. M. Barrie was later to locate his Peter Pan).
He described sitting in a glade in the park one day, experiencing a
sense of communion with the trees, flowers and birds:

---

53   Kenneth Grahame, *A Bohemian in Exile – A Reminiscencein Pagan
     Papers*, 1898.
54   Robert Frost, *Pan with Us*; see too William Ernest Henley, *The Gods Are
     Dead?* and Edward Thomas, 'The Passing of Pan,' in *Roseacre Papers*,
     1910.

"In the huge world, which roars hard by,
  Be others happy if they can!
  But in my helpless cradle I
  Was breathed on by the rural Pan.

I, on men's impious uproar hurl'd,
  Think often, as I hear them rave,
  That peace has left the upper world
  And now keeps only in the grave.

Yet here is peace for ever new!"[55]

Even in such unpromising surroundings, it was possible for the presence of the god of Nature to be discerned, as several other Victorian poets testified. Bliss Carman, for instance, detected Pan in the hurdy-gurdy player who appeared in his street one early spring day:

"There, in the springtime of the world,
  Are dancing fauns, and in their van,
  Is one who pipes a deathless tune—
  The earth-born and the urban Pan."

His 'piping' is akin to that of the Hamelin musician, with children dancing behind him down the road, and the vagrant himself is an embodiment of the god, "A smiling, swarthy, hairy man." Pan not only still lives, then, but he is alive even in city gardens and suburban parks. Wherever life is reawakened in the spring, Pan will continue to be there.[56]

---

55 Matthew Arnold, *Lines Written in Kensington Gardens*, 1849.

56 Bliss Carman, *Urban Pan;* see too W. E. Henley, *Allegro Maestoso*; James Elroy Flecker, *Oak & Olive;* Patrick Chalmers, *Pan Pipes*.

THE PAN OF POETS

As I have mentioned several times, Pan was associated with music, dance – and thence with song and poetry – primarily because of his invention of the reed pipes after his loss of the nymph Syrinx. This was a favourite story, and poets could have simply limited themselves to rehearsing it, but many sought to expand upon it and to seek new meanings and symbols.

Richard Le Galliene declared Pan "the father of poets." For James Elroy Flecker, poets were central to the revival of Pan during this era: "our poets chanted Pan/ Back to his pipes and power…" Flecker was almost definitely correct in this observation, but the poets did not merely give Pan new fashionability and currency. They gave him new meaning and vitality, extending the scope of his sovereignty.[57]

Walter Henley did just this in *Allegro Maestoso,* the title of which is taken from a musical term meaning a fast and lively tempo played in a majestic manner. He reimagined Pan as an enchanter of the natural world:

> "To the measures of his rough, majestic song;
> The lewd, perennial, overmastering spell
> That keeps the rolling universe ensphered,
> And life, and all for which life lives to long,
> Wanton and wondrous and for ever well."

Pan's music, earthy and sexy as it is, is what motivates and enlivens life.

---

57   Le Galliene, *Attitudes & Avowals,* 1910, 19.

The many other poems mentioned and reproduced here attest to the dramatic power and spiritual meaning that the Arcadian god offered. Literally hundreds of literary works concerned or referred to the deity, from poems to plays to novels to the German magazine *Pan* (published 1895–1900). A peak in output was visible between 1895 and 1918 and, by 1910, E. M. Forster commented on the fad in *Howard's End*: "Of Pan and the elemental forces, the public has heard a little too much."[58] A few years later, Max Beerbohm tackled the subject more directly. He remarked in a satire on contemporary novelists that "From the time of Nathaniel Hawthorne to the outbreak of the war, current literature did not suffer from any lack of fauns." Of the new book, *A Faun on the Cotswolds,* by fictional author Mr Braxton, Beerbohm reflected that, when the novelist had first started to write, "fauns had still an air of novelty about them. We had not yet tired of them and their hoofs and their slanting eyes and their way of coming suddenly out of woods to wean quiet English villages from respectability. We did tire later. But Braxton's faun, even now, seems to me an admirable specimen of his class – wild and weird, earthy, goat-like, almost convincing."[59]

Doubtless, in some cases (such as Mr Braxton's), the classical furniture was mere fad and show. In her short verse drama, *A Poet at the Court of Pan,* Lady Margaret Sackville suspected as much and satirised those poets who called on Pan, but would have been terrified to actually meet him. Even so, she made good use of the myth herself.

---

58 Forster, *Howards End*, 1910, c.13.
59 Beerbohm, 'Hilary Maltby and Stephen Braxton,' in *Seven Men*, 1917; see also Somerset Maugham, *Cakes and Ale*, 1930, c.11.

PAN THE GOD OF PASSION

"Pan feels the passions of love deeply engraven in his heart,
  with as fair nymphs, with as great fortune, as Apollo, as
  Neptune, as Jove; and better than Pan can none describe
  love."[60]

As nature's pre-eminent deity, fecundity lay at the heart of Pan's purpose and appeal. He is not only the God of the Spring for plants, stimulating the sap in flowers, trees and crops; he superintends the fertility of flocks and herds and, it must follow, of humans too. Walter Henley identified that Pan motivated sex – and that coupling was, in return, a celebration of the divinity:

"For lo! the wills of man and woman meet,
  Meet and are moved, each unto each endeared,
  As once in Eden's prodigal bowers befell,
  To share his shameless, elemental mirth
  In one great act of faith…"[61]

The Arcadian god is, unquestionably, a god of natural and healthy desire. Pan, himself, is constantly surrounded by nymphs, many of whom are adoring:

"Pale wood-nymphs peep'd around me whispering "Pan!"
  And sweeter faces floated in the stream
  That gurgled to my ankle, whispering "Pan!"
  And, clinging to the azure gown of air

---

60   John Lyly, *Midas*, IV, 1.
61   Henley, *Allegro Maestoso*.

That floated earthward dropping scented dews,
A hundred lesser spirits panted "Pan!"[62]

Nymphs are, of course, notoriously attractive – naked and distracting as well as amiable towards the male woodland spirits:

"the gnarled eyes of trees
Stare, big as Fauns' at Dryades,
That bend above a fountain's spar
As white and naked as a star."[63]

Even allowing for these undeniable charms, Swinburne even suggested that it was somehow innate and predetermined that Pan and his satyrs should be drawn to chasing nymphs. In a debate with the man Thalassius, he claims that what would eventually pall on a human can never cease to excite a demi-god:

"Thy feet are a man's, not cloven
Like these, not light as a boy's:
The tresses and tendrils in-woven
That lure us, the lure of them cloys
Thee."[64]

Just as Swinburne saw, nymphs are, inextricably, 'in-woven' with every myth about Pan, so it will be important to say a little more about them.[65]

---

62 Robert Buchanan, *Pan*.

63 Cawein, *Forest & Field*.

64 Swinburne, *Pan & Thalassius*.

65 See too my *Nymphology – A Brief History of Nymphs*, 2020.

NYMPHS AND THEIR WAYS –
PAN'S RETINUE

ᴘan is often represented, in art as well as in literature, as a kingly figure surrounded by a court or troop of followers. These comprise fauns and satyrs, nymphs and (sometimes) female maenads and bassarids who are, perhaps more properly, members of Dionysus' retinue but have latched onto the goat god instead.

The satyrs and fauns are almost invariably male. Female satyrs are known in art, but within Pan's orbit the creatures share the god's gender *and* his characteristics – both physical and behavioural. What attaches them to his court is the presence of female company. Young women are the other regular feature of Pan's menage; whether they are semi-divine nymphs or ecstatic humans, drawn to him by the orgiastic nature of his cult, they are present as an element that's both cohesive and disruptive. According to legend it was the oreades and dryads, the mountain and tree nymphs, who were most closely linked to Pan. The naiads and hamadryads, meanwhile, are reported to prefer to keep to themselves.

Many poets have emphasised the nymphs' desirability. American poet Madison Julius Cawein was especially taken with the physical charms of these members of Pan's entourage; as he demonstrated when he repeatedly conjured their carnal allure in richly suggestive verse:

> "As rises up, in Siren seas,
>   To rock in purple deeps, hip-hid,
>   A virgin-bosomed Oceanid.
>   Gaunt shadows crouch by tree and scaur,

Like shaggy Satyrs waiting for
The moonbeam Nymphs, the Dryads white,
That take with loveliness the night,
And glorify it with their love."

"Mænad, Bassarid, Bacchant,
  What you will, who doth enchant
  Night with sensuous nudity.
  Lo! again I hear her pant
  Breasting through the dewy glooms...
  Lo, like love, she comes again,
  Through the pale, voluptuous dusk,
  Sweet of limb with breasts of musk.
  With her lips, like blossoms, breathing
  Honeyed pungence of her kiss,
  And her auburn tresses wreathing
  Like umbrageous helichrys,
  There she stands, like fire and snow,
  In the moon's ambrosial glow,
  Both her shapely loins low-looped
  With the balmy blossoms, drooped,
  Of the deep amaracus.
  Spiritual yet sensual,
  Lo, she ever greets me thus
  In my vision; white and tall,
  Her delicious body there,
  Raimented with amorous air..."

79

In similar terms, the poet dreamed of the "beautiful nakedness" of "beautiful-bosomed" nymphs, of oreads with "slim loins" and "bewildering tresses," of dryads' "racy lips" and of "fountain lovely" naiads rising dripping from pools – but yet frustratingly possessed of "evasive hips."[66]

Nymphs are at the heart of Pan's court, and are a key motivating feature of his world, but his relationship with them is a problematic one.

---

66 Cawein, *Forest & Field; Dionysia; Dithyrambics; Loveliness; The Dryad; The Limnad; Myth & Romance.*

CHAPTER 6

Pan the God of Lust

There was very evidently considerable temptation amidst the nymphs and groves – and it is does not seem that Pan can – or could – ever resist his natural, physical urges. Both he and his companions were renowned for their tireless chasing of the nymphs. In the chorus of *Atalanta in Calydon*, Swinburne evoked the reluctance and fright that the nymphs (usually) feigned:

> "And Pan by noon and Bacchus by night,
>   Fleeter of foot than the fleet-foot kid,
>   Follows with dancing and fills with delight
>   The Maenad and the Bassarid;
>   And soft as lips that laugh and hide
>   The laughing leaves of the trees divide,
>   And screen from seeing and leave in sight
>   The god pursuing, the maiden hid.

> The ivy falls with the Bacchanal's hair
> Over her eyebrows hiding her eyes;
> The wild vine slipping down leaves bare
> Her bright breast shortening into sighs;
> The wild vine slips with the weight of its leaves.
> But the berried ivy catches and cleaves
> To the limbs that glitter, the feet that scare
> The wolf that follows, the fawn that flies."

Even American Madison Julius Cawein, whose faery visions were usually quite anodyne, acknowledged the carnality that fairytales and classic myths both share:

> "A Dryad laughed among the trees;
> A Naiad flashed with limbs a-spark;
> A Satyr reached rough arms to seize;
> A Faun foot danced adown the dark
> To music of rude pipes of bark:
> Earth crowded all its shapes-around,
> Myths, bare and beautiful of breast,
> 'Mid whom pursuing passion pressed,
> Wild, Pan-like, leaping from the ground.
> A Dryad laughed among the trees."[67]

Not to put too fine appoint on it, Pan may be described as lust personified; as Madison Cawein actually chose to do in his poem *Loveliness* – although, again, he does not fail to emphasise the sexual attractiveness of the nymphs either:

---

67   Cawein, *Wood Dreams*, 1913.

"And we may see the Satyrs in the shades
  Of drowsy dells pipe, and, goat-footed, dance;
  And Pan himself reel rollicking through the glades;
  Or, hidden in bosky bow'rs, the Lust, perchance,
  Faun-like, that waits with heated, animal glance
  The advent of the Loveliness that wades
  Thigh-deep through flowers, naked as Romance,
  All unsuspecting, till two hairy arms
  Clasp her rebellious beauty, panting white,
  Whose tearful terror, struggling into might,
  Beats the brute brow resisting, but evades
  Not him, for whom the gods designed her charms."[68]

In point of fact, so notorious were Pan's uncontrolled nympholepsy, and the general immorality of his entourage, that Lady Margaret Sackville could satirise them in wry tones:

"Here's a tale from times called olden, further qualified as
      golden,
  When the gods on high Olympus smacked of earth and
      sunburnt tan,
  With their far-from formal Dryads, and their Oreads and
      Naiads,
  And the questionable doings of the forest Courts of Pan."[69]

Richard Le Galliene likewise saw the entire court as 'lacking refinement.' Like the natural world they personified, they could

---

68 Cawein, *Loveliness*, stanza IV; see too *The Dryad*, in which Cawein refers
    to "amorous Pan.".
69 Sackville, *Daphne*.

easily offend the squeamish and the dainty. "Pan and Sylvanus and the nymphs are not respectable" he warned.[70]

PAN THE LECHER

Natural sexual urges can become distorted and pathological in some situations and, for Pan and the satyrs, the constant proximity of young females could constitute a factor that aggravated an already unrestrained and animalistic appetite. Pan, as a god, is related to Priapus and his priapism could become distinctly problematic when normal arousal turned into stalking and nuisance. Priapus (just like Pan) is associated with stories of pursuing nymphs; in his case he chased Lotis, who was transformed into a lotus flower in order to escape his amorousness.

The goaty god's constant desire could get him into trouble, as when – according to Robert Browning – he set a trap and captured Luna, the moon goddess:

> "So did girl-Moon, by just her attribute
>   Of unmatched modesty betrayed, lie trapped,
>   Bruised to the breast of Pan, half god half brute,
>   Raked by his bristly boar-sward while he lapped -
>   Never say, kissed her! that were to pollute
>   Love's language – which moreover proves unapt
>   To tell how she recoiled – as who finds thorns
>   Where she sought flowers – when, feeling, she touched –
>   horns!"[71]

---

70 Le Galliene, *Attitudes and Avowals*, 1910, 20.
71 Browning, *Pan and Luna*.

The goddess' revulsion is clear (although Browning admits of the possibility that Luna succumbed anyway) but a fundamental problem for the goat god as lover is revealed: his appetites can sit ill with his appearance – and many potential lovers are repelled. In his poem *Apollo in Pherae*, Aleister Crowley has one of the Olympians refer to the god in these terms:

> "the brutish God,
>> The disgustful animal we chafe to name
>> A God even as ourselves…"

Unfortunately, therefore, nymphs are just as prone to flee Pan as to embrace him. Oscar Wilde knew that they might be wary of him and that sometimes they would try to escape:

> "Pan, plash and paddle groping for some reed,
> To lure from her blue cave that Naiad maid
>> Who for such piping listens half in joy and half afraid."

> "Long time I watched, and surely hoped to see
>> Some goat-foot Pan make merry minstrelsy
>> Amid the reeds! some startled Dryad-maid
>> In girlish flight! or lurking in the glade,
>> The soft brown limbs, the wanton treacherous face
>> Of woodland god!"[72]

This situation was made much worse by Pan's insistent sexual harassment of nymphs. The natural response of many females therefore was to distrust, fear and flee Pan. Gordon Bottomley

---

72 Wilde, *Ravenna*, 1878 & *The Burden of Itys*, 1881.

(perhaps because he was a man) joked about the situation in his poem *The Dairymaids to Pan.* They hide in their beds and seek the protection of the young male labourers on the farm against the one they call 'Goatfoot.' They ask him to protect their herds, but to leave them well alone. Lady Margaret Sackville was a good deal less sanguine about this aspect of the god's behaviour: she has Syrinx wish desperately that "some kind god would foil/ The inexorable purpose of Pan's lust,/ Having pity on my swift youth's recoil..."[73]

Worse than their efforts to escape, the fleeing nymphs sometimes called upon the Olympian gods and goddesses to save them from ravishment by transforming them into plants: Daphne into a laurel, Syrinx into reeds. Robert Buchanan described such a scene in his *Pan:*

> "Down the long vale of Arcady I chased
>   A wood-nymph, unapparell'd and white-limb'd,
>   From gleaming shoulder unto foot a curve
>   Delicious, like the bow of Artemis:
>   A gleam of dewy moonlight on her limbs;
>   Within her veins a motion as of waves
>   Moon-led and silver-crested to the moon;
>   And in her heart a sweetness such as fills
>   Uplooking maidens when the virgin orb
>   Witches warm bosoms into snows, and gives
>   The colourable chastity of flowers
>   To the tumultuous senses curl'd within.
>   Her, after summer noon, what time her foot

---

73   See for example Sackville, *Syrinx* or John Gould Fletcher, 'The Flocks of Pan' in *The Book of Nature,* 1913.

Startled with moonlight motion milk-blue stalks

Of hyacinths in a dim forest glade-

Her saw I, and, uplifting eager arms,

I rush'd around her as a rush of boughs,

My touch thrill'd thro' her, she beheld my face,

And like a gnat it stung her, and she fled.

Down the green glade, along the verdurous shade,

She screaming fled and I pursued behind..."

As we know, this loss in love gave rise to music when Pan carved pipes from the reeds into which Syrinx had been transmuted, but humanity's gain was probably of little consolation to the frustrated deity, who was left barely consolable in some versions of the story.[74]

These justifiable fears notwithstanding, Oscar Wilde also envisaged a scene in which woodland Pan was well-enough trusted by the tree nymphs to protect them against other would-be ravishers:

"The Dryads come and throw the leathern ball

Along the reedy shore, and circumvent

Some goat-eared Pan to be their seneschal

For fear of bold Poseidon's ravishment,

And loose their girdles, with shy timorous eyes,

Lest from the surf his azure arms and purple beard should

rise."[75]

---

74   R C Trevelyan, *The Bride of Dionysus*, 1912, Act III, 2.

75   Wilde, *Charmides II*, 1881.

These lines help to redress the balance and remind us that Pan could be a caring and attentive lover as well as a molester. He was also allowed to find calm and solace in the company of nymphs. In his poem *The Naiad*, Robert Buchanan once again recognised the radiant beauty of the nymphs, describing how even wild beasts were "awed by my pale face, whose light/ Gleameth thro' sedge and lilies yellow," but he went beyond this cliché to a new vision of the relationship:

> "Oft do the fauns and satyrs, flush't with play,
> Come to my coolness in the hot noon-day.
> Nay, once indeed, I vow
> By Dian's truthful brow,
> The great god Pan himself did pass this way,
> And, all in festal oak-leaves clad,
> His limbs among these lilies throwing,
> Watch'd the silver waters flowing,
> Listen'd to their music glad,
> Saw and heard them flowing, flowing, flowing,
> And ah! his face was worn and sad!"[76]

There was one true, requited love in the god's life, and she was the nymph Pitys. In Walter Savage Landor's telling of the story, his adoration for her arose from a fight between the enraged goat god and Cupid. The mischievous boy found Pan asleep and woke him suddenly by playing on his pipes. A struggle developed between the two which Cupid ended by shooting one of his arrows in Pan's eyes. He was blinded, which Venus healed, but he proved too impatient to remove his bandages and so was punished with a doomed passion.[77]

---

76   Buchanan, 'The Naiad,' stanza 3, in *Undertones*, 1863.
77   Landor, 'Cupid and Pan, in *Hellenics*.

Landor described the love of Pan and Pitys in a companion poem. Pan competed for the dryad's attentions with the god Boreas. Pitys, in turn, doubted Pan's constancy and sincerity, suspecting him of being unfaithful with Cynthia, the moon goddess, and she teased him with talk of her love for Boreas. In truth, her preference was for Pan and, when Boreas discovered that he had lost her, he was furious and jealous. One day, he came upon the couple embracing and, falling into a vengeful rage, he hurled a boulder at the tree-nymph:

> "It smote the Dryad, sprinkling with her blood
> The tree they sat beneath: there faithful Pan
> Mused often, often call'd aloud the name
> Of Pitys, and wiped off tear after tear
> From the hoarse pipe, then threw it wildly by,
> And never from that day wore other wreath
> Than off the pine-tree darkened with her gore."[78]

The goat god faced disappointments, frustration and tragedy in his love life, but this should not distract us from the wider message of his amorous and sexual nature: that is, that genuine physical love is a natural, healthy function of the living being and is, as such, a valid form of worship of the god. Rather than repressing our carnal natures, Pan encourages us to express them openly and unashamedly.

Algernon Blackwood reflected upon this in his short story *A Touch of Pan*.[79] The events described take place over just one night at a country house party. The narrator is a young man who has

---

78   Landor, *Pan & Pitys*.
79   From *Day & Night Stories*, 1917.

become engaged to a rich heiress, merely because of her wealth and status. However, he has found himself strangely attracted to the daughter of the family that has organised the party in their stately home. She is regarded by most as "backward," unable to conform to the social conventions of the time, but he sees in this 'natural' girl something vibrant and refreshing. During the afternoon of the gathering, he slips outside into the garden and finds the girl by the statue of a satyr. As they talk, their love for each other overwhelms them. At midnight they meet again in the moonlight and are both possessed by a strangely wild and liberating spirit. They start to run through the garden and somehow become transformed into fauns (or people dressed only in close fitting furs). They hurry to a nearby grove, where other fauns and nymphs are waiting, and dance and play there like "wild children." Then, suddenly, piping is heard and a stir passes through the group as they feel "the panic of reverent awe that preludes the descent of deity." A god arrives (unnamed, but almost certainly Pan) and with him come a sense of "brimming life. Of rapture." He "sanctioned every natural joy in them and blessed each with his power of creation." The couple then decide to return to the house to spy on the other guests from outside. In contrast to "the joy of abundant, natural life, pure as the sunlight and the wind" that they had felt in the "stupendous Presence" in the wood, the guests at the party seem ugly, unnatural and devoid of innocence. The pair see their familiar world plainly and in nakedness. "Their backs were bare, for all the elaborate clothes they wore; they hung their breasts uncleanly; in their eyes shone light that had never known the open sun." There was pretence, guilt and shame. The narrator's fiancée is in the room, but leaves it with her married lover for an assignation in the garden. They too head towards the wood, for the purposes of clandestine sex. In contrast to the earlier celebration by the 'wild children' in the same wood, the refined affairs of these members of 'high society' are revealed as being nothing but unnatural vice and lust. The natural innocence of an "unruined world" prevails.

To conclude, we should further remind ourselves that Pan is the source of inspiration to poets and composers of songs. This reputation derives, of course, from his association with love (and passion) but also because of his links to burgeoning nature and the joys of life. Pan provokes the people "To utterance of fond prophetic song, / Who singing smile, because the song is sweet…" Madison Cawein took this aspect of the god further still when he praised him as the source of knowledge. The poet's lover is "adorable and wise" and this is because "the woods among, / She met with Pan, when very young, / Who taught her all his lore" – what Cawein elsewhere termed "the mysteries of the woods."[80]

THE GAY GOD

For the Victorians, Pan's unbridled heterosexual activity was shocking enough, but during the later nineteenth and early twentieth century a particular aspect of his conduct was brought to the fore by certain British poets and authors. This was his potential as a gay icon. The Greeks accepted unhesitatingly that Pan would sometimes seduce young shepherds in addition to the nymphs he chased. This was wholly unremarkable to them, but within British society towards the end of the Victorian era, the repression, secrecy and shame enforced upon gay men was

---

80 Buchanan, *Pan;* Cawein, *Pupil of Pan, Wood God* and *Dreamer of Dreams*.

considerable. Anything that indicated that a different approach to homosexuality was possible was seized upon by those who felt oppressed and excluded by social attitudes.

Pan sometimes appeared in the Greek myths as a ridiculed outsider, but he was also the god of nature – and in classical times it had not been felt contradictory to this status for him to wish to have sex with boys; indeed, 'to honour Pan' was a phrase used as a euphemistic reference to gay sex. Victorian men with the same desire could therefore draw considerable comfort from the thought of a culture where their sexuality was treated as normal. A succession of works was produced which alluded, generally very subtly, to the homo-erotic aspects of Pan worship.[81]

The poetic celebration of gay identity through Pan came after a period during which scholars (mainly in Germany) had revived the study of ancient Greek culture, treating the evidence for homosexual relationships as a historical fact that had to be examined without moral judgment. These studies had given a certain sober respectability to discussions of the "unspeakable vice of the Greeks." This in turn created an avenue by which the issues could be taken up more generally. That said, the common representation of the god with a large erection – indicative of his role of the source of life – will not have gone unremarked. In the Greek pantheon, Pan was sometimes thought to be the father of Priapus, another god of fertility who was known for his outsized and continually erect penis. Pan as the masculine deity of sexual enjoyment for its own sake, and unshackled from the institutions

---

81 In recent years several studies have been devoted to this aspect of the modern Pan cult. I will not endeavour to repeat what has already been handled better and more fully elsewhere. I give a brief outline here and direct interested readers to Victor Imko, *Pan and Homosexual Panic in Turn of the Century Gothic Literature*.

of marriage and parenthood, may therefore have added to his appeal as a gay icon.

Oscar Wilde is, of course, remembered as a gay martyr, but his use of the classical god was amongst the most restrained of his contemporaries. Pan is mentioned conventionally as the source of poetic inspiration in *The Garden of Eros*:[82]

"And I will cut a reed by yonder spring
  And make the wood-gods jealous, and old Pan
  Wonder what young intruder dares to sing
  In these still haunts..."

Pan's also mentioned affectionately by Wilde, along with "brown Satyrs in a jolly crew", Bacchus, Apollo and others, in *The Garden of Itys,* whilst nymphs and satyrs appear throughout his verse, a reflection of his easy familiarity with the classics.[83] Nevertheless, Wilde's double villanelle, *Pan,* is a much more personal and direct invocation of the god. Rather than using his name as erudite decoration, the poet calls on the deity to revive a lost world of freedom and joy:

"... O goat-foot God of Arcady!
  Ah, what remains to us of thee?

  Ah, leave the hills of Arcady,
  Thy satyrs and their wanton play,
  This modern world hath need of thee.
  No nymph or Faun indeed have we,

---

82 See too *Phedre, Canzonet* and *Ravenna* of 1878.
83 See, for example, *The Sphinx, Charmides, Endymion. Panthea* and *In the Forest.*

For Faun and nymph are old and grey,
Ah, leave the hills of Arcady!
This is the land where liberty
Lit grave-browed Milton on his way,
This modern world hath need of thee!
A land of ancient chivalry
Where gentle Sidney saw the day,
Ah, leave the hills of Arcady.
This fierce sea-lion of the sea,
This England lacks some stronger lay,
This modern world hath need of thee!
Then blow some trumpet loud and free,
And give thine oaten pipe away,
Ah, leave the hills of Arcady!
This modern world hath need of thee!"

Other male writers more deliberately emphasised some of the sexual aspects of Pan's character and were, generally, more homo-erotic in their prose. Representations of Pan tended, at the same time, to become younger and – perhaps, more effeminate – more boyish, beardless and pretty. Peter Pan, anomalous as he is in the period's literature, does share this trait with the other Pans of the time.

In his *Story of a Panic*, published in 1912, E. M. Forster described events surrounding a holiday picnic in the Italian Hills. The party are speculating whether or not Pan had been driven from the local woods when suddenly a silence falls, fear seizes the group and they flee back to their hotel in the nearby town; all except a boy of fifteen, Eustace, who is left behind. When his absence is noticed, the adults return to the hillside to search for him, fearing the worst. He is found safe and well, but strangely changed. Goat tracks surround the spot where he is discovered.

Returning to the hotel in Ravello, Eustace becomes suddenly and closely attached to a local boy working as a waiter there. This sudden and intimate bond with Gennaro seems to be due to the fact that he has shared the same experience as Eustace on the hillside. Then the English boy suffers some kind of breakdown: he can't sleep in his hotel room because he feels trapped, cut off from nature, so he runs off into the darkened garden. Gennaro is used to lure Eustace back inside, but he again becomes hysterical and has to be locked in his room. Gennaro sets his new friend free and he runs off into the night again – leaving Gennaro to seemingly have to die in his place. Eustace discovers his true nature through Pan and, as a result, is liberated into a new life.

Pan is only allusively present in this short story. He is a more threatening and real presence in E. F. Benson's *The Man Who Went Too Far* (1912). A monstrous goat has been sighted in a wild and ancient part of the New Forest. Meanwhile, Frank, an artist, who is living alone in a cottage in this same area, has embarked upon a mission to become at one with nature. He seems to be succeeding, as he grows mysteriously younger. A friend called Darcy who visits Frank is amazed by his physical as well as spiritual transformation. There's a clear, but discrete, homosexual tension between the two: Darcy describes Frank as a "glorious specimen of young manhood" and he tells him "You have bewitched me, you extraordinary boy." He is much less convinced by his friend's 'fairy tales' about Pan, though. Frank says he has heard pipes playing in the forest; at first, he was scared, but now he hears them regularly without fear – even though he knows that when he sees Pan, he is likely to die. In due course, he is discovered dead – trampled by a goat in a kind of orgiastic communion and sacrifice. It appears that Frank's mistake had been to be too incautious, too familiar towards the god. He rashly wanted union with Pan, without considering the danger inherent in the natural world. He was punished for his hubris.

The most explicit of these 'gay Pan' stories is Forrest Reid's *The Garden God – A Tale of Two Boys* (1906). Two fifteen-year-olds, Harold and Graham, spend a summer holiday together before returning to school. "This place and this weather are pleasant enough for Pan," Graham exclaims. As a younger boy he had fantasised about playing with a handsome Greek God in his garden. During this idyllic holiday Graham doesn't need make-believe because he has Harold as his companion. Looking back from old age, he recalls his friend's "shapely body;" having him pose naked after swimming, in "all his wonderful beauty," like "A Faun! A young woodland Faun!... [but] You are far nicer than the statue." The pair pray together to Pan and make an offering to him, but their burgeoning summer romance is cut short when Harold is killed by a bolting horse – perhaps a victim of 'panic.' He is taken by the god and so remains ever young.

Reid dedicated his novel to Henry James, who was apparently scandalised by the unwelcome gesture – and severed contact with him. James appears very likely to have struggled with his own repressed homosexuality throughout his life and could have found association with an account of two boys being physically close very uncomfortable. Perhaps it was in response to just such repressive social attitudes that Laurence Housman composed his 1896 story, *When Pan was Dead*.[84] Housman espoused a variety of controversial views and life styles. He was a socialist, pacificist, supporter of women's rights and member of the Order of Chaeronea, a secret society that promoted a new homosexual ethos in ethics and culture. The Order's founder George Ives

---

84 Housman, in *All Fellows – Seven Legends of Lower Redemption*, 1896.

declared that "We believe in the glory of passion. We believe in the inspiration of emotion. We believe in the holiness of love." This could all be found encompassed in the cult of Pan, explaining its attractiveness, but the criminal law of the time demanded circumspection – hence the form of Housman's parable.

When Pan Was Dead concerns a 'woodling,' a brown-skinned, long-haired nymph, who wakes from hibernation to find that she is all alone in the world after all her other 'wood-mates' had died over winter. She seeks the friendship of the women living in a nearby convent, first of all befriending a lay sister who does all the chores for the cloistered nuns. The woodling brings the unhappy sister 'wood-dreams' of the spring woods, the sunshine and human company – and she soon deserts the convent. Having lost one companion, the woodling decides to put on the lay sister's abandoned habit and to perform her work so she can bring happiness to the other women. As an innocent creature of nature, she can't comprehend the life of privation and self-denial being lived by the nuns; she finds their religion painful and cruel. She puts "roots of sweet relish" in their meals, but this leads only to tears and grief. She brings flowers and greenery into the convent, but this gives rise to temptation, for which the nuns have to do penance by scourging themselves.

The woodling finds it deeply unnatural for the nuns to choose pain over pleasure, so she decides to drug them with mandrake. The nuns go into a frenzy and run out of the convent naked into the moonlight. Once again, the wood is full of "nymph-like bodies" bathing in the stream and "beautiful maenad laughter" echoing around the trees. Dawn finds the twelve pale figures (and one brown one) dancing and singing on a hillside. There they are encountered by a shepherd and his flock. The response of the woodling is just to laugh and to jump like a squirrel into a tree;

the nuns emit a lamentable cry and scatter in shame and horror. The woodling rings the convent bell to call them back together, but she realises that her plan to help has failed. She leaves them to their guilt and suffering and joins the mandrakes in the soil.

By allusive analogy, Housman criticises the repression of the bodily urges demanded by the church. Our incarnation should be a source of pleasure, not of guilt, something the pagan spirit of nature is able to express.

CHAPTER 7

Pitiless Pan

The corollary of a deity who represented the elemental forces of nature was that he could be experienced by humankind not as a positive force of pleasure and joy, but as harsh and cold.

IMPERSONAL PAN

In 1912 Irish novelist James Stephens published his fairy story for adults, *The Crock of Gold*. It is a very strange tale, in which philosophical musings are matched with more whimsical, even bizarre, adventures involving leprechauns and fairies. The god Pan appears too, alongside the Irish god the Angus Óg.

Pan's portrayal is intriguing. He comes as a liberator for a country girl called Caitilin Ni Murrachu. She is a remarkably beautiful girl who no longer finds her rural life satisfying. She senses there is something more awaiting her – and one day Pan, the Master of Shepherds, arrives. He tells her that he has come to her because he had to do so, just as the bee goes to the flower. His philosophy is simple: "You must not do anything because it is right, but because it is your wish." "Love is the shaggy beast that goes down," diving below thought and wisdom. Caitilin is unable to resist him: he seems sad and grotesque but, when he smiled, "it was as though the sun shone suddenly in a dark place, banishing all sadness and gloom."

Pan is the god of pure instinct. With him, "Love is unclean and holy" and life is careless and happy. As god of nature, he demonstrates to her the redundancy of clothes, and she wanders around gloriously naked. For Pan, determining what is right or wrong may be "the beginning of knowledge... but it is not the beginning of wisdom." Life is very simple: "it is to be born, and to die, and in the interval to eat and drink, to dance and sing, to marry and beget children." Virtue, he says, "is the performance of pleasant actions" whilst vice is to neglect to perform them. When the man called The Philosopher comes to try to rescue Caitilin, Pan tells him that philosophy only leads to the sin of sterility. Repression and self-sacrifice are lauded as honourable when, in fact, they are suicide.

Simultaneously, though, Pan does not guide or advise; he does not teach or dictate. He simply is, being and living, but without aim or purpose, relying solely upon his senses. When the handsome young god Angus arrives, Pan does not try to persuade Caitilin not to leave with him. He does not argue or resist. He simply goes with the flow of events, accepting and accommodating whatever she feels is right for her.[85]

85   Stephens, *The Crock of Gold*, cc.6, 9, 10 & 12.

ELEMENTAL PAN

The impersonal aspect of Pan, exemplified in the previous example, can assume a more dangerous quality when we view him as an expression of the natural processes of the world. As Robert Louis Stevenson already observed, storms, lightning, floods and landslides do not have a moral aspect; they are simply physical forces that operate as the laws of gravity, physics and meteorology necessitate.

Knowing his many guises, as haunter of glades and hunter of maids, Madison Cawein mused over the nature of the god, asking "What art thou and these dim races,/ Thou, O Pan, of many faces,/ Who art ruler yet?" The poet felt that an important part of the answer lay in his manifestation through the wilder forces of nature and that the essence of the god lay in his awesome power coupled with an ability to soothe:

> "Once in tempest it was given
>   Me to see thee, where the leven
>   Lit the craggy wood with glare;
>   Dancing, while – like wedges driven-
>   Thunder split the deeps of heaven,
>   And the wild rain swept thy hair.
>   What art thou, whose presence, even
>   While with fear my heart was riven,
>   Healed it as with prayer?"[86]

Pan may be found in "the naked and nymph-like feet of the dawn," but he can just as much be seen at work in storm-tossed seas,

---

86   Cawein, *Pan*.

raging winds, howling wolves and volcanic eruptions. The god is present "in all things evil and fearful that fear may scan,/ As in all things good, as in all things fair that fall." Both happiness and tears proclaim and prove the god's existence. He's the lord of "ravin and ruin" as fully as he's the lord of life and light. He is, by nature, changeable, but this can mean as swift a change back to light as the plunge was into darkness.[87]

Life concludes with the natural process of death, of course, and Pan is death. In his 1906 poem *Sorcery,* Walter de la Mare describes hearing the voice of the god crying to him. He wants to follow, but a woodman advises him *not* to seek to see Pan's face. Nonetheless, the sweet, sad singing draws him on: "I dreamed his eyes to meet,/ And found but shadow laid/ Before my tired feet."

POWERFUL PAN

The loving and respectful awe that Pan evoked in Mole and Ratty in *Wind in the Willows* could very easily shade into a holy terror and dread in the face of his divine powers. The poem *A Nympholept,* by Algernon Swinburne, captures this sense of god-fearing worship. The narrator is in a wood on a hot summer noon. The wind that stirs is the word of the god, like a flame that runs:

"Creative and subtle and fierce with invasive power,
    Through darkness and cloud, from the breath of the one
    God, Pan."

---

87 Swinburne, *A Nympholept;* see too Madison Cawein's *Fallen Beech,* in which the rain and wind are compared to a faun's hooves and Pan's pipes.

The narrator senses his "immanent presence, the pulse of thy heart's life" and calls on the god to have mercy, "For I know thee well,/ How sharp is thine eye to lighten, thine hand to smite." The fierce midday both reveals the god's mercy and conceals his wrath. It is for these reasons that Pan can provoke panic equally as well as rejoicing.

Pan can be a vengeful god too. Swinburne described how severely he chastens those who trespass against him with panics and that:

> "Man
> Knows well, if he hears beside him
> The snarl of thy wrath at noon,
> What evil may soon betide him,
> Or late, if thou smite not soon,
> Pan."[88]

In *The Music on the Hill*, a story from 1911 by Saki, a woman who shows disrespect to Pan pays sorely for her offence. Sylvia Seltoun is a new arrival in the remote rural town of Yessney. She's told that the worship of Pan still survives there, but she boasts that she's not such a fool as to believe in an ancient god. Out walking, she steals an offering of grapes placed before a bronze statue of a youthful Pan in a copse, meaning to eat them herself rather than letting them go 'to waste.' She's warned that "the Wood Gods are rather horrible to those who molest them" and, sure enough, Pan revenges himself for her scepticism. Out on another walk, she hears the sound of a pipe and then sees a young gypsy boy she'd seen before near the statue. Then Sylvia confronts a stag that is

---

88   Swinburne, *Pan & Thalassius*.

fleeing a hunt. In its panic, it charges her, although at the moment the antlers strike, she hears only the "echo of a boy's laughter, golden and equivocal." Saki's story is strongly anti-female, but he correctly identified a trait in the Greek pantheon as a whole: they are always prepared to punish those who fail to show due reverence, who are blasphemous or who displayed hubris – as in Benson's *The Man Who Went Too Far*, discussed earlier.

Pan can also be vengeful because he feels despised or excluded. As we know, nymphs may flee him simply because of his looks and their revulsion is often compounded by mistrust of his intentions. Rape is too real a possibility, which makes Pan's contacts with the nymphs a matter of anxiety and – very probably – further encourages his insecurity and his hastiness. Repeatedly we hear of this – for example:

> "A Hamadryad, haply, who,
>   Culling her morning meal of dew
>   From frail, accustomed cups of flowers,
>   Now sees some Satyr in the bowers,
>   Or hears his goat-hoof snapping press
>   Some brittle branch, and in distress
>   Shrinks back..."

> "An Oread who hesitates
>   Before the Satyr form that waits,
>   Crouching to leap, that there she sees?"

> "Then satyrs and the centaurs passed:
>   And then old Pan himself; and there,
>   Flying before him, all her hair
>   About her like a mist, the last

Wild nymph I saw; and as she went
The woods as with a wind were bent."

"Haunter of green intricacies…
  Where the shaggy Satyr chases
  Nymphs and Dryads, fair as Graces,
  Whose white limbs with dew are wet…"[89]

Understandably, this repeated experience of rejection can breed an inferiority complex. Aleister Crowley imagined Pan describing himself dismissively, bitterly contrasting himself with more handsome gods:

"I drag my hoofs in the clay. I do not fashion
  Songs for the stars upon a golden lyre-
  I … scrape out rough tunes
  On common reeds. I am not beautiful,
  I have not eyes like June-blue heavens on fire,
  Nor hair filched from the harvest of the sun,
  Nor a white matchless shape, supple and swift
  And strong and splendid. I am an earthy thing,
  Half goat and half coarse boor, not fit to touch
  The sun's moon-sister…"[90]

In *The Satyr*, Robert Buchanan examined the emotions of the half-human being at length. To a large extent, the poem's satyr seems to have internalised others' view of him; he refers to himself as "a hybrid like me/ Goat-bearded, goat-footed" who is fit only to use a rough tree trunk as a pillow. He seems dismissive of his

---

89 Cawein, *Forest & Field; Dionysia; Wood Myths; Pan.*
90 Crowley, *Apollo in Pherae.*

pastimes, describing how he spends his time in "rude riot:" he runs and shouts all day with his fellows and with the god Silenus, becoming drunk until:

> "I stagger after
> The wood-nymphs fleet,
> Who with mocking laughter
> And smiles retreat;
> And just as I clasp
> A yielding waist,
> With a cry embraced,
> Gush! it melts from my grasp
> Into water cool,
> And – bubble! trouble!
> Seeing double!
> I stumble and gasp
> In some icy pool!"

Rejection and mockery are his lot, deservedly, because he is noisy, coarse and uncouth. Sometimes he has caught a nymph who has crept too near to him and "Kiss'd her, caress'd her-/ Ere she scream'd, and flew." This is all entirely understandable to the satyr, because he has seen his reflection in pools and he knows that he is monstrous: "Goat-footed, knock-kneed,/ A monster, indeed,/ From horns to hoof." In summary, he seems resigned to the fact that he is seen as "A thing wild, unholy,/ And foul to the seeing;" the satyr is inferior, repulsive and uncivilised. In Buchanan's verse there is redemption in a sense of harmony with nature; however, the easier and more predictable response is to feel vengeful.[91]

---

91 Buchanan, 'The Satyr,' in *Undertones,* 1863.

Buchanan, in his poem *Pan*, took the goat god's resentful emotions to a logical, but nevertheless surprising, conclusion. Pan is, he complains "Goat-footed, horn'd, a monster – yet a god." The discrimination and the deprivations he feels that he has suffered rankle with him. Instances of his prejudicial position are easy to recall – such as when he chased the gorgeous nymph Syrinx, and the gods intervened to turn her into reeds so that she might evade him. He is "Pan the scorn'd" and so he prophesies vengeance:

> "In the time to come…
> Some law more strong than I, yet part of me,
> Some power more piteous, yet a part of me,
> Shall hurl ye from Olympus to the depths,
> And bruise ye back to that great darkness whence
> Ye blossom'd thick as flowers; while I – I, Pan—
> The ancient haunting shadow of dim earths,
> Shall slough this form of beast, this wrinkled length,
> Yea, cast it from my feet as one who shakes
> A worthless garment off; and lo, beneath,
> Mild-featured manhood, manhood eminent,
> Subdued into the glory of a god,
> Sheer harmony of body and of soul,
> Wondrous, and inconceivably divine."

It seems that, in Buchanan's vision, Pan becomes the very deity who displaces all the former gods of Greece and Rome. He is the fulfilment of those predictions of his death.

Another revenge of Pan might be upon the forces of modernity which are devastating the natural world. Lord Dunsany's story *The Prayer of the Flowers* suggests how the protective role granted to him by Kenneth Grahame in *The Wind in the Willows* might become something more proactive.[92] The narrator is standing at night between two railway embankments on the edge of a city in the English Midlands. He is surrounded by factories, noise and pollution. The flowers cry out to Pan:

> "The woods have gone away, they have fallen and left
> us; men love us no longer... Great engines rush over the
> beautiful fields, their ways lie hard and terrible up and
> down the land... The woods are gone, O Pan... And thou
> art far, O Pan, and far away."

Pan hears the flowers' voices on the west wind and replies reassuringly from Arcady: "Be patient a little, these things are not for long." Quite what Pan might do was imagined by R. K. Ensor in his poem *Pan in the Pennine,* of 1903. He finds his creatures being poisoned by smoke and resolves:

> "I must go pray the silver-tinkling Rain,
> To deaden with its drops that drip of tears,
> Remit the pangs of witnessing that pain,
> Let for a little while my world be mine again."

Pan then summons all the forces of nature to purify the world – washing away the corruption and (hopefully) giving humanity a second chance.[93]

Algernon Blackwood's brief tale, *Ancient Lights,* might also be read as a practical illustration of what Pan will do. A surveyor is sent from Croydon down into rural Sussex to inspect an old

---

92 In Dunsany, *Fifty-One Tales,* 1915.

93 Ensor, in *Modern Poems,* 1903; others saw that it was man's duty to do the
    work, such as John Cowper Powys, in 'The Faun,' in *Poems,* 1899.

copse of oak and hornbeam that a landowner wishes to cut down to improve the view from his house. The little wood seems to be alive, surrounding and misleading the man, tripping him up and instilling a real terror. He glimpses two little figures in browny green who laugh as they bodily eject him from the enclosure, which, it turns out, is called Fairy Wood. We may regard this pair as fairies, wood sprites or the spirits of the trees themselves. Whatever their exact nature, they use force and fear to achieve their purpose.[94]

PAN THE GOD OF MADNESS

We should not forget an aspect of the god which is now so familiar that we are not even aware of his presence when we mention it: that is, Pan's ability inspire fear verging upon madness. We refer, without reflecting upon etymology, to 'panic' and to 'panic attacks,' scarcely noticing the god's implied influence in these losses of control. The older psychological term, 'panophobia' more explicitly emphasised the influence of the god upon the human mind.

Pan symbolises an aspect of human nature we might rather obscure. Author Sir Osbert Sitwell said that in the First World War "Pan and Mars had broken loose together and had set out to conquer... civilised living." The goat god underlies mental as well as sexual excess; he may be present in our poetic imagination, but also in our nightmares and in our psychological disturbances.[95]

---

94 Blackwood, 'Ancient Lights,' in *Ten Minute Stories*, 1914.

95 See William Faulkner's short story, *Black Music* (1934), for an interesting example of temporary 'possession' by Pan.

EVIL PAN

As I shall examine in more detail in the following section, classical representations of Pan provided the model for the Christian church's conception of the appearance of the devil. So synonymous have these two images become, in fact, that the characters of the goat god and Satan have coalesced and it has become possible to ascribe to Pan all the evil and insurrection that traditionally goes with the figure of the fallen angel Lucifer.

It will be clear that the Greek god has a clearly defined character and that aspects of his behaviour may seem antagonistic towards humankind. Nonetheless, he cannot be conceived of as an epitome of all evil. Unfortunately, that has not stopped the name Pan being used as a shorthand for Satan and he was able, for some Victorians and Edwardians, to become a convenient symbol for everything that was monstrous, nightmarish or, simply, threatening.

The Edwardian age saw a boom in writing about supernatural and fantastic subjects and Welshman Arthur Machen was at the forefront of this. Machen was a fine writer of fantasy and horror; unfortunately, in his short novella *The Great God Pan*, he used the currently fashionable name of the Greek god to add piquancy to his plot. Published in 1894, the story concerns the consequences of an ill-fated scientific experiment. A Dr Raymond has been studying for years how to reach "the real world... beyond this glamour and this vision, beyond the ["dreams and shadows" of the visible world], beyond them all as beyond a veil." He believes that "the ancients knew what lifting the veil means. They called it seeing the god Pan." Despite the huge gulf between these two dimensions, he has realised that he could bridge it with only the very slightest brain surgery and he has decided to perform this intervention with a young ward of his, a girl called Mary. She, for the first time ever, will gaze upon the spirit world and see Pan face to face. In fact, the operation goes horribly wrong: the girl awakes in convulsions from the terrible sights she has witnessed. She has become a "hopeless idiot" and dies within the year.

A couple of decades later, a series of strange deaths take place in London society. They are all connected to a mysterious woman called Helen Vaughan, who is said to be beautiful and, yet, to have something utterly repulsive in her expression. It slowly emerges that she is Mary's daughter, born after the terrible visions induced by the surgery. Helen has been profoundly affected by this prenatal experience and (it appears) she introduces her acquaintances to her infernal companions, causing them to die of fright or to commit suicide in appalled despair at the "most awful, most secret forces" that are disclosed to them, forces that cause their souls to "wither and die and blacken." Eventually Helen is confronted and is forced to destroy herself, ridding the world, as it were, of a portal to hell.

A very similar view is taken of Pan in Machen's masterpiece of 1907, *The Hill of Dreams*. At the start of the book its hero, Lucian, becomes lost one very hot summer's day. He discovers himself in a strange landscape whilst walking near where he lives in South East Wales. "All afternoon his eyes had looked on glamour, he had strayed in fairyland ...like the hero of a fairy-book." Lucian follows an unknown lane "hoping he had found the way to fairyland" and then scrambles up to an overgrown Roman fort that crowns a hill overlooking his home. He is alone on this 'fairy hill' and feels drowsy in the sweltering heat, seeing the twisted trees turn into human shapes and "the gleaming bodily vision of a strayed faun." The wood seems alive and Lucian hears "the old wood-whisper or ... the singing of the fauns." The boy strips off his clothes and falls asleep in the sunlight. When he awakes, he has the impression of dark eyes, scarlet lips that kissed him, and a visitor who dashes away. Lucian flees the wood in an ashamed panic, filled with feelings horror and defilement.

However, when he later thinks back to the afternoon, Lucian at first feels "a swell of strange exultation." This is directly related to the fact that, later the same summer, the youth becomes bewitched by a beautiful young local woman called Annie, who speaks "wonderful, unknown words" – apparently an unintelligible, possibly fairy, language. She dismisses her speech as "only nonsense that the nurses sing to the children" but it becomes apparent that there is more to it than that – that it is, in fact, some form of enchantment. Lucian falls morbidly in love with her for a time.

It is not clear whether, when he slept that afternoon on the "hot soft turf," he dreamed of seeing a faun, or of becoming one, or whether this actually took place. Be that as it may, Lucian increasingly comes to feel that he has witnessed a "horrible sabbath" and has been subject to black magic with the result that "he had never come out [of the wood in the fort] but a changeling had gone down the hill, and now stirred about the earth." Over the coming years, Lucian is unable to settle and spends more and more time alone and detached from reality, uncertain whether he has been subjected to a spell or even has fairy blood in his veins. He moves to London, but cannot escape the impact of the fauns' incantations in the wood.

The visit to the old fort seems to have resulted in Lucian's possession by satyrs, nymphs or witches. He slowly realises that he was surrounded that afternoon by unknown figures – a woman who had watched him "between the matted boughs and her awful companions, who had never grown old through all the ages." The hideous shapes in the wood continually "called and beckoned to him," all of which culminates in a terrible vision in which Lucian returns to the wood on the hill. Hideous shapes swarm in the thickets. He is drawn inexorably to the heart of the fort for an infernal rite or orgiastic wedding. It is revealed that his village girlfriend Annie is the Queen of the Sabbath and a mistress of witches. Accompanied by a horrible old woman, naked, she is no longer "the symbol of all mystic womanhood" and his beloved; rather – alarmingly – "jets of flame issued from her breasts" and she drinks his soul, consummating his ruin and death.

Once again, as in *The Great God Pan,* fauns and satyrs are not symbolic of natural vigour and exuberance but rather of a cloying and corrupting evil. Machen embraces the image of Satan as a half goat being; the sexual frenzy associated with him is perverse and soiled. There may even be, in the description of Lucian's experience in the sun-baked grove, an echo of the hints of homoerotic carnality that we saw earlier in the work of E. M. Forster and E. F. Benson. Nonetheless, Machen seems to have seen only sin here, not release and the opportunity to express the real self.

One other work by Machen is worth noticing. This is his short story *The Terror,* a horror-mystery of 1917, which is concerned with a revolt by nature against humanity. It is a comment upon the barbarity of the First World War and imagines domesticated animals turning upon humans in imitation of the humans' barbarity to each other. It might be considered as a variation upon the theme of Pan's revenge upon us for our pillaging of nature.

Somerset Maugham portrayed another demonic Pan in his novel, *The Magician* (1908), a story which is primarily an extended parody of the beliefs and practices of Aleister Crowley. The goat god appears in a vision as:

> "a monstrous, goat-legged thing, more vast than the
> creatures of nightmare. She saw the horns and the long

113

beard, the great hairy legs with their hoofs, and the man's rapacious hands. The face was horrible with lust and cruelty, and yet it was divine. It was Pan, playing on his pipes, and the lecherous eyes caressed her with a hideous tenderness."[96]

The Pan/ Satan of Machen's stories owes a great deal more to the 'Old Nick' devil of British folktales than to the myths of the classical god and the author's admixture of gothic horror had a considerable impact on future generations. The devil of *Rosemary's Baby* or the works of Dennis Wheatley are the descendants of Machen's seminal stories.

Part of Machen's skill as a writer of horror is that he never directly described the monsters of his stories. We only have hints from which to construct our own nightmare. In fact, most of the Pans of late Victorian and Edwardian literature are only ever glimpsed, or are detected only by their hoof tracks – it is part of their mystery and part of their power. The murderous Pan of Saki's *Music on the Hill* is seen fleetingly and indistinctly as a young boy; his voice or his pipes are frequently the primary evidence of the god's presence. It's perhaps only in *The Garden God* that there's a clearer vision of a naked, muscled form – but that's because it's part of a young boy's sexual fantasy.

The Pan at the heart of the nineteenth century cult was unusual, then: he was powerful and ever present, but he was also invisible. In this, it might be argued, he was quite unlike a classical god, but exactly like the Christian god with whom he contended. Perhaps his power was augmented by this very absence.

---

96   Maugham, *The Magician*, 1908, c.8.

CHAPTER 8

Modern Pan

The core image of Pan as a god of desire has persisted into modern era, but at the very start of the twentieth century artist Aubrey Beardsley offered a novel slant upon the theme. In his unfinished novel, *Under the Hill,* which appeared in 1904, Beardsley offered a highly decadent and strangely contemporary take on Pan and his entourage.

In the course of his narrative, Beardsley describes the plot of an imaginary play, *The Bacchanals of Sporion,* which is a comedy ballet in one act. Allegedly, the Marquis de Vandésir was present at the first performance and left a short impression of it in his *Mémoires.* The events are set in a secluded Arcadian valley where, to the music of pipe and horn, a troop of satyrs are first seen making offerings of nuts, green boughs, flowers and roots upon an altar to the "mysterious Pan." They are then joined by shepherds and shepherdesses from the hills in a ritual dance to the music of a choir of children.

This innocent and harmonious scene is immediately followed by the arrival of the youth Sporion, who is accompanied by a brilliant rout of dandies and smart women in sumptuous and elegant clothes. Sporion is described as a tall, slim and depraved young man. He and his friends are tired of the amusements offered by the civilised world and have invaded Arcadia in the hope of experiencing a new frisson through the destruction of some shepherd's or some satyr's naïveté, and by infusion of their venom among the dwellers of the woods.

Slowly, and warily, the fauns and shepherds emerge from their hiding places, lured by the strange looks, by the scents and the drugs, and by the brilliant clothes, of Sporion and his companions. They dance together and then the sylvans are offered champagne, with the intruders "plying those Arcadian mouths that had never before tasted such a royal drink." The result is inevitable:

> "'Twas not long before the invaders began to enjoy the first fruits of their expedition, plucking them in the most seductive manner with their smooth fingers, and feasting lip and tongue and tooth, whilst the shepherds and satyrs and shepherdesses fairly gasped under the new joys, for the pleasure they experienced was almost too keen for their simple and untilled natures. Sporion and the rest of the rips and ladies tingled with excitement and frolicked like young lambs in a fresh meadow. Again and again, the wine was danced round and the valley grew as busy as a market day."

All this noise and the merrymaking attracts the children who had formed the choir earlier. In a flash Sporion disentangles himself and springs to his feet, gesticulating in delight, because he is so fond of children:

"Scarcely had he caught one by the thigh than a quick rush was made by everybody for the succulent limbs; and how they tousled them and mousled them! The children cried out; I can tell you. Of course, there were not enough for everybody, so some had to share, and some had simply to go on with what they were doing before."

After a while, Sporion and his friends grow tired and exhausted with their new debauch:

"they cared no longer to take the initiative, but, relaxing every muscle, abandoned themselves to passive joys, yielding utterly to the ardent embraces of the intoxicated satyrs, who waxed fast and furious, and seemed as if they would never come to the end of their strength. Full of the new tricks they had learnt that morning, they played them passionately and roughly, making havoc of the cultured flesh, and tearing the splendid frocks and dresses into ribands. Duchesses and Maréchales, Marquises and Princesses, Dukes and Marshalls, Marquesses and Princes, were ravished and stretched and rumpled and crushed beneath the interminable vigour and hairy breasts of the inflamed woodlanders. They bit at the white thighs and nuzzled wildly in the crevices. They sat astride the women's chests and consummated frantically with their bosoms; they caught their prey by the hips and held it over their heads, irrumating with prodigious gusto. It was the triumph of the valley.[97]

---

97   Beardsley, *Under the Hill,* 1904, chapter 4.

Events have degenerated into a pansexual orgy. This, in itself, is not especially novel, perhaps – although at the time Beardsley's allusive references to a spectrum of sexual activities, including child sex, were probably very shocking. The key novelty of the text, though, is the artist's suggestion that the woodland beings have been corrupted by the humans. This takes the natural and innocent sexuality of the satyrs and nymphs and twists it. Eden is polluted by human sophistication.

NEW VISIONS

During the twentieth century, to a considerable extent, Pan was subsumed within a wider conception of a divinity. In 1933, Egyptologist Margaret Murray published *The God of the Witches*, in which she advanced the idea that Pan was merely one form of a horned god who had been worshipped across Europe by a witch-cult. Her theory had a strong influence upon emerging the Neopagan notions of a horned god symbolising male virility and sexuality that were being elaborated by figures such as Gerald Gardner and Dion Fortune. Pan is more likely now to be referred to by the Celtic name of Cernunnos.

It has also been argued that, following the First World War, Pan as god of nature no longer seemed to offer solutions to societies' woes and worries. The destruction of the natural world, exemplified by the pulverised landscapes of Northern France and Flanders, alongside the human costs of the conflict, seemed to leave no space for a pastoral deity. The end of the war in 1918 is presented by some commentators as a cut-off point in the literature of the Pan cult – and certainly some of the poets who had formerly sung his praises (Rupert Brooke and Joyce Kilmer, for instance) died on the Western front. Nevertheless, poets, novelists and artists continued to make use of him as a potent symbol.

Even so, after the war spiritual reassurance was frequently sought elsewhere: some people reverted to the spiritualism that had been popular in the previous century; others, such as Arthur Conan Doyle, also found hope in fairies, following the emergence of the Cottingley fairy photographs. It might be recalled that in a 1917 poem Robert Graves had declared the fauns 'out of season,' but it should be noted that the previous year in *Premature Rejoicing*, poet Edmund Blunden still managed to imagine Titania, the fairy queen, in occupation of a shattered wood on the Somme battlefield and resurrecting the greenery after the war. It might be argued, of course, that these faes are just another manifestation of the spirit of nature, and that the fundamental yearning was exactly the same.

Whilst he may have been transmuted in new age belief, Pan has continued to fascinate and entertain us in popular culture. Fauns appeared in Disney Studios' animated film *Fantasia* (1940), which is based on Beethoven's Symphony No. 6 (1808). They were drawn with brightly coloured legs and hair (yellow, pink, mauve and blue) and they play pipes and cause mischief. The fauns seem to be young boys and, as such, lack the sexuality of the classical archetype, but they still help cupids to pair up male and female centaurs.

A faun, Mr Tumnus, appears in the *Narnia* books by C.S. Lewis, primarily in *The Lion, the Witch and the Wardrobe* (1950) but briefly later in *The Horse and His Boy* and *The Last Battle*. Lewis recorded that the first Narnia story came to him from a single mental image of a faun carrying an umbrella and parcels through a snowy wood. Lewis described this faun as having ruddy skin, curly hair, brown eyes, a short, pointed beard, horns on his forehead, hairy goat legs with hooves, a "strange but pleasant little face" and a long tail. Tumnus also, rather effetely, has a scarf and an umbrella and lives in a cave furnished with carpet, armchairs and a bookcase. He is said to be not much taller than the eight-year-old human child, Lucy Pevensie, whom he befriends after she enters Narnia through a wardrobe. Tumnus is a very good example of the emasculation of the satyr that took place over the twentieth century. By rights, he should have been chasing Lucy around Narnia; instead, he harmlessly invites her home for boiled egg, sardines, toast and sugar-topped cake.

Beyond these works designed for children, adult interest persisted in the mythology of Pan. An illustration of this may be found in the September 1950 edition of *Fate* magazine, in an article *Ancient Rites of Pan* by Frank Patton.[98] It is illustrated by fairly typical scenes of Pan cavorting with naked women and satyrs. Patton recognised that there were really three Pans: "a minor character, a mere puppet in a greater sideshow; a mask for the more vicious and characterless god, Dionysus; and the most important of all the *earthy* gods." As the drawing heading the piece indicated, Pan is often shown sitting in a woodland glade engaged in one of two pursuits – playing his pipes, or pursuing nymphs. Secondly, he's associated with the orgiastic excesses of the resurrected god Dionysus. Thirdly, he has a continuing relevance as a spirit of nature and natural processes.

The reading of the classics had not entirely waned either. For example, in 1977 poet and playwright James Reeves published a slim volume of *Arcadian Ballads,* which was illustrated by Edward Ardizzone. These verses were adaptations of Ovid's *Metamorphoses* and included the familiar story of Syrinx. She is

---

98   Patton, 'Ancient Rites of Pan, *Fate,* vol.3 no.6, Sept, 1950, 41–44.

a slim, virtuous and chaste woodland nymph who, because she is also "sinuous and wild" is easily able to outpace the "satyrs and spirits of the wood" who'd like to ravish her. However, one day she meets a "shaggy form and face," Pan, "the forest god, and lord amongst the pines." She feels sudden fear of this goat-foot god and flees. He pursues her, begging for an embrace "to sate his goatish greed" and the naiads save her in the reed bed, as we know.

ECO-PAN

The most significant development in Pan's persona was both scientific and spiritual. Scottish scientist and author Robert Ogilvie Crombie (1899–1975) was a modern adherent of this latter aspect of the Pan cult. Born in Edinburgh, he trained as a scientist but found that poor health made regular employment very difficult. Eventually, he retired to the countryside near Perth to get closer to the natural world and developed ideas about spirituality and ecology that had a formative influence upon the Findhorn Foundation.

During the early 1950s Crombie (who was usually known as ROC) had several encounters with the spirit world whilst still living in Edinburgh. His first was in the city's Botanic Gardens, where he saw a three-foot-high faun called Kurmos. The faun was very surprised to discover that ROC was able to see him – as most humans could not – and they had a friendly conversation which led to Kurmos visiting ROC's flat. Crombie was to see Kurmos again in the Gardens but his next major encounter took place not long afterwards in Princes Street, in the heart of the city. Walking home one evening, ROC met the great god Pan himself. He was very tall, but ROC felt not apprehension but affinity with him. Pan was friendly and played his pipes to the man.

About ten years later, in May 1966, ROC was visiting Iona when he met Pan again. The god said that he wanted to help mankind, even though they were abusing the natural world. He described to Crombie how he was a universal, cosmic energy and could assume any form he chose. Pan's half man, half goat appearance represented the fact that he combined both intellect and animal energy. He also explained that, to work with plants, he needed an etheric body which could take on 'thought forms.'

A few months later, in September 1966, ROC was attending a conference at Attingham Park just outside Shrewsbury. Walking in the grounds there, he met Pan again and the god 'possessed' his body so that the two were united and ROC was able to look at the world through the god's eyes. He then saw that the woods around him were full of elementals, nymphs, dryads, fauns, elves, gnomes and fairies. These beings ranged in height from almost microscopic dimensions to three to four feet high. Some were dancing, some swarming and some were working with the plants. Pan then played his pipes and danced inside ROC's body.

In 1972 ROC had a further vision in the Edinburgh Botanic Gardens. It was Midsummer Eve and he saw Kurmos again, along with elves, gnomes and a tree spirit. He realised that his purpose, or mission, was to reconnect people with the nature spirits so that the world could survive and recover from the depredations that mankind was inflicting upon it. This realisation was expressed subsequently in his work with the Findhorn community.

The experiences of Ogilvie Crombie express a new vision of the supernatural world that's quite distinctive of the later twentieth century. At the very same time, fairies and other nature spirits, first recognised by the Theosophists, Rudolf Steiner and Geoffrey

Hodson, were being imbued with a similar urgent function: to save the world from pollution and exploitation.

D. H. Lawrence had contributed something to this new philosophy in his 1926 essay, *Pan in America,* in which he asserted humanity's co-existence in a shared universe with plants and animals.[99] The author returned to theme two years later in *Lady Chatterley's Lover,* in which he posited Pan, or a pagan spirituality, as an alternative to the dissatisfactions of capitalism, and the consumerism that it fuels it:

> "We've got this great industrial population, and they've got to be fed, so the damn show has to be kept going somehow... Their whole life depends on spending money... That's our civilization and our education: bring up the masses to depend entirely on spending money... If you could only tell them that living and spending isn't the same thing! But it's no good. If only they were educated to live instead of earn and spend, they could manage very happily... if they could dance and hop and skip, and sing and swagger and be handsome, they could do with very little cash... They ought to learn to be naked and handsome, and to sing in a mass and dance the old group dances, and carve the stools they sit on, and embroider their own emblems. Then they wouldn't need money. And that's the only way to solve the industrial problem: train the people to be able to live and live in handsomeness, without needing to spend... They should be alive and frisky, and acknowledge the great god Pan.

---

99   Lawrence, 'Pan in America, in *South West Review,* vol. 11, no. 2 (January, 1926), 102–115.

He's the only god for the masses, forever. The few can go in for higher cults if they like. But let the mass be forever pagan.

But the colliers aren't pagan, far from it. They're a sad lot, a deadened lot of men: dead to their women, dead to life... Money poisons you when you've got it, and starves you when you haven't."[100]

Lawrence's twentieth century Pan is a god of the natural human pleasures, just like his classical predecessor, but he's also a god of self-sufficiency, simplicity and traditional communities. He's a quasi-communist, arts and crafts deity who, in the tradition of William Morris and Edward Carpenter, wants to re-vision both work and society. Nearly a century later, there are still powerful arguments for such an approach: indeed, they may be more pressing now than they were in the 1920s.

Ogilvie Crombie's work, meanwhile, gave existing affinities and concerns a freshly messianic emphasis: a benign oversight of nature had to become actively interventionist to avert disaster. Sadly, of course, these messages are still as relevant as they were fifty years ago, but more acutely urgent. The messengers, regrettably, still seem like fringe figures.

---

100   Lawrence, *Lady Chatterley's Lover*, 1928, c.19.

PART THREE

Portraying Pan in the Arts

This section of the book considers how Pan has influenced music and, most particularly, the fine arts.

The iconography of Pan is significant for several reasons. Firstly (as mentioned before), the ancient concept of the faun or satyr was commandeered by the Christian church for the representation of the devil, creating for Western audiences deeply engrained responses to representations of beings with horns and hooves. This imagery at the same time fed back into native British beliefs, helping to give form to Robin Goodfellow and Puck in the seventeenth century and, in due course, contributing to our notions of fairies with pointed ears.

Secondly, Pan, fauns and satyrs have, in themselves, provided a rich source of inspiration for Western painters. The juxtaposition of semi-human beings and naked nymphs, all enriched by suggestions of sex, were irresistible subjects for successive generations of painters and sculptors, as we shall see.

The history of representing Pan in the fine arts is long and distinguished. It is interesting to note, however, that in the middle of the nineteenth century it was (briefly) thought that the new art of photography might supplant such old themes. One enthusiast felt that it was high time to move away from the hackneyed subjects of painting: "wearisome nudities called Nymphs and Venuses... its dead Christianity and its deader Paganism." Fresh ideas, fresh ideals and new artists would sweep this all away, it was predicted. This didn't happen, of course, and still in the twenty-first century, painters and other graphic artists are creating images of the horned god.[101]

---

101 *Photographic Journal,* February 21st 1857, 217.

CHAPTER 9

Painting Pan

Pan, his satyrs and nymphs have long been a fascination of artists –
for obvious reasons. This chapter will examine the presentation of
the god and his companions over the centuries, but it is worthwhile
noting that the deity can be present in artworks without the need
for actual representation.

British painter Paul Nash was only a very young and aspiring
artist in September 1911 when he first came across the Wittenham
Clumps in Oxfordshire. He was visiting a cousin at Sinodun
House near Wallingford when, out walking one day, he discovered
the Clumps and instantly fell under their spell. He wrote to his
friend Mercia Oakley:

> "The country about and about is marvellous – Grey
> hollowed hills crowned by old, old trees, Pan-ish places
> down by the river wonderful to think on, full of strange
> enchantment... a beautiful legendary country haunted by
> old gods long forgotten."

Nash returned a year later and drew the trees for the first time. In his 1936 autobiography, *Outlines,* the artist recorded the impression they made upon him that summer day:

> "There was one aspect which had I the wit to perceive
> it, would convey the strange character of the place, one
> image, which in its form would contain the individual
> spirit."

The image of the trees on their isolated hilltop remained with him for rest of his life and the last series of pictures he painted, showing the phases of the moon, featured the Clumps as a focal element in their composition. Throughout his career, indeed, Nash was fascinated by the idea of a *genius loci,* a spirit of place, at ancient places such as Avebury, Maiden Castle and Silbury Hill. Sketching at the last location, Nash sensed "the true yield of the land... identical with the intimate spirit inhabiting these gentle fields..." Perhaps we could also call that spirit Pan – the face glimpsed between the leaves, the figure flitting through the trees.

This spirit within the British landscape continues to be celebrated into the present day, through the work of artists such as the members of the Brotherhood of Ruralists, Graham Arnold, David Inshaw and Graham Ovenden, and painters of the more recent Arborealist group, including Paul Newman.

RENAISSANCE PAN

At first, Renaissance art was church art, as had been most public art of the Middle Ages. Although the 'rebirth' was concerned with rediscovering classical culture in all its forms, the science, philosophy and literature as well as art, it was at first only intellectually that the Greek and Roman gods were considered. Italian humanists explored the works of the Neo-Platonist thinkers and sought to reconcile the classical pantheon with the Christian trinity, finding parallels and analogies. Leon Battista Alberti (1404–72) enabled these currents to gain visual form. He was a typical Renaissance polymath, writing on science, mathematics, architecture and the theory and practice of the arts. In his book 'On Painting' (circulated first in Latin in 1435 – *De Pictura* – and then in Italian in 1436– *Della Pittura*), Alberti argued for the application of the laws of perspective to painting and recommended that mythological subjects should properly be chosen by artists for their narrative works. Oddly, it was not until the 1470s the painters responded to the licence they had received from Alberti. Then, in 1475, Poliziano depicted the 'Realm of Venus' in his *Stanze per la Giostra* and soon afterwards the trend blossomed famously in the work of Alessandro Botticelli. His *Primavera* (1477–8), *Pallas and the Centaur* (1482), *Mars and Venus* (1483) and the *Birth of Venus* (1484) are now internationally recognised and are regarded as typical of his style. In fact, he only turned to classical themes over ten years into his career and for him they were very much a side-line to his main business in portraits and religious paintings, such as endless pictures of the *Madonna and Child*.

For our purposes, the most significant Renaissance work was probably Piero di Cosimo's *Mythological Scene,* which is now in London's National Gallery. In this Di Cosimo (1462–1521) produced what Michael Levey has called "a masterpiece of interpretation." By this he means that nobody knows for certain what the picture shows. A satyr is kneeling near a sea shore beside a dying nymph, who has a wound in her throat. A mournful dog sits nearby and others prowl on the beach in the background.

Whether they might be responsible for the fatal wound is unclear; who the characters are is equally unclear. The painting is dated to about 1495 and is sometimes called *The Death of Procris*, perhaps inspired by Ovid's account in *Metamorphoses* VII of a young woman's death at the hands of her jealous husband Cephalus. A play based on the story, *Cefalo*, was written by Nicola da Correggio and first performed in 1487. A faun featured in the text and so may have inspired di Cosimo.[102]

Whatever the exact inspiration, this tragic figure is our first true post-classical faun. He gazes at the dying girl bewildered and helpless, his loins swathed in a modest animal skin robe. He has very elongated, almost donkey like ears, dark curly hair and a little goatee beard. The nymph wears attractive golden sandals and is partially draped in rich cloths; she has the petite juvenile breasts typical of her kind. It is an enigmatic but compelling scene.

In 1499 Piero was commissioned by Giovanni Vespucci in Florence to paint a pair of companion pictures: *The Discovery of Honey by Bacchus* and *The Misfortunes of Silenus*, both of which were derived from Book III of Ovid's *Fasti*, or *Book of Days*, which had very recently been published. Both pictures are a riot of mythological beings, featuring both male and female satyrs, infants and, even, a baby faun being breastfed. Every age and description of the species is depicted.

Like Piero in these pictures, subsequent artists of the Renaissance, Mannerist and Baroque schools largely adhered to the recommendations of Alberti and sought to locate their depictions of Pan and satyrs within known incidents from classical myth. For instance, Luca Signorelli's *School of Pan*, which was

---

102   Levey, *A Concise History of Painting, from Giotto to Cezanne*, 1968, 114.

probably painted during the late 1480s or early 1490s, showed (it was destroyed in Berlin in May 1945) Pan seated amongst his followers, whom he is teaching to play reed pipes.

Several other stories involving Pan were popular: the interaction between the rough god of lust and the goddess of love was one. In Antonio da Correggio's *Venus and Cupid Discovered by a Satyr* (1528) we see an early example of a theme that will become very familiar – the satyr as voyeur. Here he raises a blue robe that is covering the sleeping goddess so that he can have a good look at her naked body. A number of other artists also tackled such scenes, one of the most unusual of which is probably Dirck Quade van Ravesteyn's rendering of about 1602, in which Venus and Cupid are being carried on the shoulders of two satyrs.[103] A related pairing, of Pan and Cupid, is also sometimes seen: the small boy fights and overpowers the goat god in an allegory of the power of love and a reference to Pan's passions for Syrinx and Pitys. Federico Zuccaro tackled the incident in about 1600 whilst an anonymous Italian painter portrayed *A nymph on the back of a goat with Pan and Cupid looking on,* a scene heavy in sexual innuendo.

Considerable mythological interest was offered by the story of the musical contest between Apollo and Pan. When King Midas preferred Pan's pipes over Apollo's lyre, he was cursed with a pair of donkey ears by the latter. Jacob Jordaens (1593–1678) tackled the topic three times; understandably, perhaps, it was also handled by Sebastiano Ricci, Jan Breughel and Jacob de Backer (1555–91). An outlier in this genre is Peter Paul Rubens' *Pan and Ceres* of 1620. This appears to be a pairing of deities with no mythological foundation, but this work (painted in collaboration with Frans Snyders) makes symbolic sense in that it unites the

---

103   See too paintings by Giorgione, Giovanni Biliverti and Filippo Lauri.

d with the goddess of cultivation. Van Dyck provided a
bination, *Diana and a Nymph Surprised by a Satyr,* but
lly a 'voyeur' scene, with the satyr cautiously reaching
na's robe away from her lap.

Far surpassing all other subjects in popularity was Pan chasing
the nymph Syrinx. Peter Paul Rubens handled the story several
times – his *Pan and Syrinx* of 1577 has the goat god on the point
of capturing the well-rounded nymph, who finds herself trapped
on the margin of a reedy pool. She cries out to the Olympian gods
for salvation. Hendrik van Balen the Elder's 1615 *Pan Pursuing
Syrinx* is nearly identical, as is that by Flemish painter Jordaens.[104]
The same painter's pictures of a *Satyr Playing Pipes* stand as
harbingers of another very popular Pan theme.[105]

A final popular scene was the seduction of princess Antiope by
Zeus, who took the form of a satyr to win her over. Images of the
pair are common, but it can often be hard to know whether or not
the male depicted is the Olympian god or simply a sylvan. Van
Dyck painted the incident, as too did Cornelis van Poelenburgh,
Jordaens, Corregio, Titian, Rembrandt, Nicholas-Pierre Loir and
Goltzius. One attraction of the scene, perhaps, was the fact that
Antiope could be painted as very young, an aspect of nymphs
which was to become increasingly noticeable.

Very quickly, however, artists of the period realised that Pan
and his cohorts could simply offer convenient vehicles for pictures
that were amusing or even titillating. Rubens painted several other
scenes which are just excuses to show revelry or seduction – *The
Drunken Satyr* or *Satyr and Bacchante* for instance. Drink can, of

---

104   Other examples were painted by Pier Francesco Mola, Pierre Mignard,
      Bon Boullogne, Sebastiano Ricci, Giovanni Grimaldi and Paolo de
      Matteis.

105   See too, Paulus Moreelse's *Pan Playing His Pipes*.

course, easily lead to sex and the Bolognese brothers Agostino and Annibale Carracci (1557–1602 and 1560–1609 respectively) are particularly notable for their indulgence in such work. Annibale's *Venus Inebriated by a Satyr* is a fairly mild example of voyeurism combined with alcohol. The brothers' work got far more explicit – indeed pornographic – so we may also enjoy a number of etchings by Agostino of fauns and nymphs copulating (one is called *The Cult of Priapus)* as well as a rather strange BDSM scene in which a satyr whips a nymph he has tied half way up a tree. There is a peculiar eroticism in Agostino's *Mason Satyr*, whose titular subject stands over a naked girl who is sprawled wantonly on a bed, raising one corner of the bedclothes to reveal a cat beneath. The satyr is holding his mason's plumb line over her groin; why he needs to find the vertical we don't know, although the he wears a small mason's apron, which only just covers his bulging erection.

The Carracci brothers produced many variations upon these basic ideas of naked nymphs being spied upon or molested, but they also painted more respectable mythological scenes, such as Annibale's fresco of *Pan and Diana* at the Palazzo Farnese in Rome (1597–1602) or his panel showing Pan asleep, holding his pipes, painted in 1592 for Cesare d'Este's Palazzo dei Diamanti. Several times, the brothers also both tackled the more traditional *Pan Conquered by Venus*, an image that referred to the story of Pitys.

To conclude, a refreshing contrast to these carnal representations is found in Gerard von Honthorst's 1623 picture, *Satyr and Nymph*. This is a portrayal of genuine affection; the pair smile lovingly at each other, the nymph tugging on his beard whilst he tenderly strokes her face.

ROCOCO PAN

Moving into the late seventeenth and eighteenth century, the established Pan themes were repeated – nymphs chased by satyrs, voyeur satyrs and such like.[106] French Baroque artist Nicolas Poussin (1594–1665), who spent most of his working life in Rome, offers us an already familiar *Nymph and Satyrs*, in which the robes are pulled off the sleeping female to expose her naked flesh to contemplation, and an agitated *Pan and Syrinx* (one of several he painted on this subject). His *Nymph, Satyr, Faun and Cupid* shows the girl being carried off on the satyr's shoulders, but rather than an abduction, they seem to be heading out for a picnic, amply supplied with wine and grapes. Italian artist Francesco Mancini (1679–1758) tackled Cupid fighting Pan in a lively way, with the winged child clambering over the goat god like a naughty toddler; the adult Pan could surely throw him off if he chose to exert his physical strength – but he is overwhelmed by something other than muscle power.

Poussin's *Triumph of Pan* is a far more interesting picture than the group with Cupid just described, as it could conceivably depict a slightly later stage of that same outing. We see revellers who are crowned with wreaths of ivy and vine leaves who appear to be rather the worse for wear, with the festivities beginning to descend into a free-for-all orgy. Watteau's *Festival of the God Pan* (c.1715) is a somewhat more restrained version of a similar event. The centre of the frame is taken up with some tranquil

---

106   For example, see renderings of *Pan and Syrinx* by Louis Dorigny, Jacopo Amigoni, Jean Francois de Troy and Noel Coypel. Johan Heinrich Keller, Francesco Fontebasso, Poussin and Ricci all tackled a *Nymph & Satyr* and *Pan & Apollo* and *Venus & Pan* were painted by Jacques Charlier, Tiepolo, Mattys Terwesten, Ricci and by an artist in Poussin's school.

musicians, whilst satyrs and naked nymphets listen calmly from the side-lines.

French painter Francois Boucher is renowned for his suggestive portraits of young women and female courtiers. His mythological scenes are in the same vein. His *Pan and Syrinx* (National Gallery, 1759) offers us not one, but two, plump young nymphs being surprised by the god. A 1743 version of the same scene rearranges the figures somewhat, but is equally devoid of the alarm and action the story ought to suggest. There is more dismay shown at the sudden grab made by Pan in the 1762 version of the incident that's to be seen in the Prado. Boucher has doubled the number of additional nymphs as well, enhancing the erotic intertwining of female limbs considerably. A further circular version, one of a pair of panels showing *Pan and Syrinx* and *Alpheus and Arethusa,* heightens further the sensual effect with Pan apparently disputing with a satyr over the right to enjoy Syrinx, who is sprawled across her lover's lap. Boucher also painted a typically luscious *Jupiter and Antiope,* another subject which remained popular with painters of the time.[107]

Lastly, two artists kept the spirit of the Carracci brothers alive. Parisian Nicolas-Andre Monsiau (1754–1837) did so with a couple of explicit oils of satyrs having sex with nymphs. Curiously, in both images he spices up an already lively scenario by adding an additional nymph to the group. In one painting she waves what appears to be a palm frond over the embracing couple; in the other she holds a garland over the head of the satyr as he squeezes her companion's breast and thrusts between her thighs.

107　See other examples by Watteau, Antoine Coypel, Poussin, Charles Van
　　　Loo & Charles le Mettais.

Meanwhile, in England, cartoonist Thomas Rowlandson (1756–1827), besides his satirical drawings and engravings of everyday life, produced a large number of erotic prints. Most of these are depictions of his fellow citizens having sex, but a few employ classical themes. *Diana, Her Nymphs and Satyrs* shows the goddess and her retinue being ogled naked by two horny satyrs; *Wood Nymphs – The Discovery* is a similar scene, with a young male (possibly human) enjoying the sight of the two girls lying naked and entwined. As ever, the combination of nudity plus a hint of post-coital slumber added immensely to the prints' attraction.

PAN IN NINETEENTH CENTURY ART

The status of Pan and his cohorts as an excuse for ribald humour, nudity and sex had been firmly established and, during the nineteenth century, most attempts to 'justify' such works by reference to a classical myth were largely (but not entirely) abandoned.[108] Most images were to be enjoyed for their own sake alone; they were often little more than slightly learned titillation. The pinnacle of this vision of the nymph might be *Les Oreades* by French academician, William Bouguereau (1902). He is an artist who always enjoyed displaying as much naked female flesh as possible but, in this canvas, he surpassed himself, depicting a swarm of over three dozen entangled and ecstatic nymphs swooping and soaring over a mountain pool, watched by three stunned satyrs.[109]

---

108   See, for example, Carl Nielsen's *Pan & Syrinx*, Laurits Tuxen's *Pan & Apollo* or *Pan & Venus* by Hans Caspar Pohm.

109   Contrast Bouguereau's *Nymphaeum* of 1878, featuring a mere thirteen nude nymphets.

The last paragraph notwithstanding, we should also observe that pagan thinking had a more serious impact upon the fine arts in the form of the Symbolist movement. The practice of magic by groups such as the Golden Dawn gave fresh prominence to the importance of signs and symbols, as well as introducing to new audiences the images and myths of ancient civilisations such as Egypt. Symbolist painting was a product of these intellectual currents, its core aim being to offer intimations of the true nature and meaning of life beyond the surface reality of the everyday world. One example may be the illustrations of William Thomas Horton, an artist strongly influenced by his friend W. B. Yeats. Other symbolists we shall consider here include Ker Xavier Roussel, Arnold Böcklin and Franz von Stuck.

During this century, a fairly standard set of subjects emerged for Pan, his satyrs and nymphs. Playing pipes and dancing were frequently portrayed, as for example in John Waterhouse's *A Hamadryad,* Dane Hans Nikolaj Hansen's *Faun Playing Pipes in a Forest* or a considerable number of paintings by Arnold Böcklin and Franz von Stuck.[110] Böcklin's *Pan with Dancing Children* (1884) shows the dark brown god surrounded by a circle of pale, naked infants as he plays. Aubrey Beardsley's *Pan and Wood Nymphs* is a delightful black and white print of the nymphs dancing in a circle, whilst holding a floral garland, to the accompaniment of his pipes. Sir Edward Burne-Jones took a slightly different view of Pan's music: in his *Garden of Pan* (1886), Pan is a slender youth whose piping seems to comfort or entrance a young, naked couple. Arcady has become like Eden in this vision of the deity. A very similar mood is created by Sydney Long in his strange work, *The Spirit of the Land of Australia* (1898). Here, Pan pipes to two

---

110   See too William de Morgan's *Pan* or Paul Paede's *Pan with Nymphs.*

naked nymphs reclined before him whilst another pair dance with two satyrs. The gum trees surrounding the glade look strangely Arcadian.

Far more popular, though, were scenes involving nymphs.[111] Satyrs spying on sleeping beauties remained popular – for example, William Etty's *Nymph with Satyrs* of 1828, *Nymph and Fauns* by Swede Julius Kronberg or Böcklin's *Fauns and Sleeping Nymph* (one of several such he painted). Passive voyeurism was nowhere near such fun to portray as something livelier and more active, though. Chasing nymphs was fun for fauns, as in von Stuck's *Faun und Nymphe,* but it was better still to catch them. What followed varied. There are pictures of what seem to be abductions and assaults-for instance Alexandre Cabanel's *Nymph and Faun* and Julian Russel Story's *Satyr and Nymph;* in Aime-Nicolas Morot's *Satyr and Nymph* it is unclear how willing the nymph is – she seems to be attempting to push him away, albeit not wholly convincingly – or perhaps her resistance is weakening after a prolonged struggle with her molester. Even so, it should be recognised that the nymphs are not always the hapless victims. Arnold Böcklin's 1874 picture, *Nymph Riding on Pan's Shoulders,* literally shows her with the whip hand. She has grabbed one of his horns to steady herself as she leans back to beat his flanks with some sort of wand.

There are also tender loving moments, such as canvases titled *Pan with a Nymph* by Otto Biermer or Eduard Veith and several pairs of fauns and nymphs portrayed by Hans Makart; there are scenes of post-coital ease, such as Arnold Böcklin's *Nymph and Faun* of 1871. Lastly, there are some unashamed depictions of

---

111   See also 'Nymph and Faun' by Ernst Josephson, Emanuel Phillips Fox
        and Albert Beck Wenzell (the latter called 'Flirtation) and Konstantin
        Makovsky's 'Nymph and Satyr.'

vigorous consensual sex. In Franz von Stuck's *Scherzo* the faun is playfully licking his partner's armpit; in his *Faun and Nymph* they are seen lying contentedly side by side in a glade; Wilhelm Truebner depicted a centauress in the passionate embrace of her satyr lover. Bavarian painter Heinrich Lossow undoubtedly painted the most memorable picture of this genre. His work regularly featured adult content: *Her Faithful Servant* showed a butler in a variety of sexual positions with his employer; his *Leda und Schwann* is a passionate avian rape and *The Sin* (1880) shows a monk taking a nun from behind through an iron gate. *Pan and Nymph* surpasses all of these for its rendering of full-frontal nudity and unashamed sexuality.

Suffice to say, these kinds of titillating scene were extremely popular – with the public *and* with artists themselves for their own amusement. Joseph Mallord Turner, for instance, filled a number of pages of his *Academy Auditing Sketch Book* of 1824 with scenes of 'satyrs at play' and 'nymphs and satyrs.'

The object of the lust of Pan and his satyrs could often be quite young. *Faun and Nymph* by Austrian Anton Romako (1832–89) shows a nymph sat on her partner's lap. He appears to be mature and slightly bald; she is a slight young teen with small breasts. The reclining nymph in Fritz Schluckmuller's *Pan with a Nymph* is a comparably youthful girl with very pert round breasts. Paul Paede's *Faun Playing the Harp* contrasts the rather ugly brown faun to two milky white young teenagers with smiling girlish faces and juvenescent bosoms. The nymph of Han's Makart's *Pan and Flora* is an even younger girl with the merest hint of a budding bosom; appropriately, the god accompanying her is just a boy too. It is worth recalling that, in spiritual terms, one aspect of Pan is to represent the vitality, renewal and regrowth of spring. However, in many of these pictures, a deliberate contrast is made between the aged, deeply tanned, shaggy and ugly half-man and the ivory pale flesh, slenderness and pubescent bodies of the nymphs. Their pearly glow and blonde tresses seem very consciously opposed to the swarthiness and muscularity of their lovers, thereby highlighting the 'interspecies' nature of their relationships – and possibly making some more profound comment upon the racial and sexual politics of the artists' own times.

Although the usual image of Pan and his male followers is one of predation – the incessant chasing and semi-rape of nymphs – Victorian painters were prepared to reverse the balance of power and to show the males overwhelmed by the females. For example, in paintings by William-Adolphe Bouguereau and Jules Scalbert, the satyrs seem to be unwilling partners in the nymphs' plans. Scalbert shows several groups of dryads forcibly dragging the males into a woodland glade where a dance is circling a statute of Pan. Scalbert's *Three Graces Dancing with a Faun* is a closely related image, but because the faun is reduced to a small boy, he seems a harmless and willing participant, wholly under the control of the older females.

A few of these nineteenth century paintings depart from the standard Pan imagery. In 1771 Goya painted an intriguing *Sacrifice to Pan*, which shows two Roman women offering bowls of wine to a more than life sized sculpture of the deity. Also unusual is Emile Foubert's *Satyr and Travellers* – a puzzling vignette of a satyr family sharing a meal with some weary gypsy types; it bears some resemblance to Baroque painter Johann Lis' *Satyr and Peasants*, an interior scene in which the presence of a mythological figure in the household seems to occasion no surprise at all.

In Franz Stuck's *Pan Watching Centaurs* the god sits on a rock at the shoreline as a male and female centaur gallop past and two merfolk stand in the shallows. Von Stuck also painted the curious

Faun and Nixie of 1918, which is set on a beach. The sylvan is wading shin deep in the waves, carrying the petite bosomed nymph on his shoulders. Arnold Böcklin painted an even odder encounter: *Two Fishing Pans* are seen raising their net from the sea and discovering, with mixed surprise and delight, that they have hauled in a mermaid. Sergey Solomko's 1904 picture of a *Mermaid and Faun* is a fourth example of such bizarre collisions between otherwise completely unrelated legendary characters.

Lastly, two pictures portray an incident in which Pan gives counsel to a lovelorn Psyche. Ernst Klimt's *Pan Comforts Psyche* of 1892 shows the goat god as old and extravagantly bearded; he is seated on a fur robe and offering sage advice to the winged young nymph. Austrian painter Alexander Rothaug also tackled the encounter: his kindly Pan is huge and shaggy – especially when compared to the slender, downcast nymph.[112] Comparably tranquil in mood is Beardsley's *Pan Reading to a Woman by a Brook;* this literary Pan is a rather effete looking young man, crowned with grapes and vine leaves: he is definitely not a god likely to roughly carry off his listener. At the other extreme, Pan was shown as an aged – and perhaps rather melancholy – god, by Russian painter Mikhail Vrubel. His 1899 *Pan* is rather shabby and unkempt, like a tramp, and gazes at us with a resigned and miserable expression, as a crescent moon sets behind him. This rather wan Pan seems to no longer have any place in the world – an image rather at odds with the god's actual standing at that time.

French painter and academic Rodolphe Julian (1839–1907) offered another view of the goat god. In his painting *Pan* the deity is portrayed as a middle-aged male, human in all but his two curved horns. He is sat amidst a group of nymphs, who are

---

112   For this story, see Thomas Sturge-Moore's *Pan's Prophecy,* 1904.

seemingly fascinated by his ability to tell fortunes from their palms. This prognostication is a traditional feature of the god, but his ordinary human legs are not. Nonetheless, it's notable that a trend existed in art, from at least Nicolas Poussin, to depict satyrs as human-like, albeit deeply tanned and with exaggerated or animalistic features. As already mentioned, Paul Paede favoured this style, as did Schluckmuller and Albert von Keller (*Faun and Nymph*, 1869).

Pan as the pastoral god was not forgotten. Johann Baptist Hofner's 1832 *Satyr with Animals* has the young faun stroking a sheep's head and with chickens, pigeon and a cat gathered companionably around. Arnold Böcklin's *Faun and Whistling Blackbird* portrays another scene of natural harmony. The satyr is seen lying beneath a bush; he has laid aside his concert flute and (bizarrely) his sheets of music and is whistling along with the bird perched on a branch above him. In *Faun with Goat* Ludwig Knaus shows a small faun boy headbutting a kid – indicating a natural affinity and interaction between equals. *Jeux des Faunes*, by French painter Louis-Eduard Rioult, depicts a similar intimacy: a young faun dances with a little goat to the sound of pipes. By contrast, *Three Fauns and a Cow*, by Swiss artist Rudolf Koller (1828–1903) is rather more puzzling and violent: the fauns seem to be trying to catch the beast – one has been thrown down, another desperately grips its tail and tries to hold its head. A calf watches from a distance, alarmed. The group are on a patch of broken land between cliffs and the shore of a stormy sea, so perhaps the fauns are trying to save it from the rocks and waves.

PAN IN THE TWENTIETH CENTURY

During the twentieth century, the popular view of the goat god softened and became more civilised. Some of the older themes may still be seen: Auguste Leroux's *Satyr and Nymph* depicts a classic scene of the sleeping nymph observed and Ernest Procter's *Bacchanal* celebrated nudity, wine and sexual licence. Carlos Schwabe's *Faun* of 1923 is a memorably vigorous and masculine image. A huge and hairy satyr, with spiralling ram's horns, bends low as he plays his pipes – possibly enchanting the foliage around him.

All the same, a quieter note seems to have prevailed. Anton Marussig (1868–1925) painted a companionable inebriation in his *Faun and Nymph* of 1918. British painter Gerald Fenwick Metcalfe presented Pan as the god of bewitching music, his pipe playing entrancing a group of nymphs gathered around him. The Australian artist, Rupert Bunny (1864–1947) had portrayed something very like this in *Pastoral* (1893). A group of figures are seated on the sea shore. One plays a pipe and the others, nymphs, satyrs and some oceanids emerging from the lapping waves, listen in rapt and reflective silence.[113]

In addition, a new sensibility emerged. As was often the case in the literature of the time as well, Pan often got much younger and much more attractive (for instance, Pole Wlastimil Hofman's *Lost Happiness* and *Whistling* (1917), in which the fauns are young boys). Often, too, a solitary figure is depicted – as for example, in Hofman's wistful *Spring* or Lithuanian painter Stanisław Bohusz-

---

113   See too pictures entitled *Faun* by Hugo Vogel, 1907 and by J. Scott Williams, *Nymph and Satyr* by Francesco Longo Mancini or *Romantic faun* by Frigyes Friedrich Miess.

Siestrzeńcewicz's *Little Faun*, in which the youthful creature sits alone at sunset in a rather desolate landscape. French cartoonist Georges Redon (1869–1943) also depicted childlike fauns, although in his satirical and parodic works they often stood in for adults. In his 1912 series of menu designs, *The Seven Deadly Sins*, 'Envy' is represented by a small faun spying on a little girl kissing a young boy on his cheek. In the saucy drawing *La Sacrée Butte*, a faun is brandishing a highly phallic banana at a little girl, whilst a sudden gust of wind whips up her dress about her waist to reveal her apparent want of knickers. There is a small hill in the background, surmounted by a windmill, but I don't think at all that this is the 'sacred mound' to which the title of the picture slyly refers.[114]

Carl Pluckebaum (1880–1952) was a German genre painter who specialised in charming pictures of little blonde girls picking flowers and generally looking coy and irresistible. His fauns are of a piece with this sugary style: they are plump endearing toddlers who appear with Christmas baubles and teddy bears. We are very far from Lossow's priapic Pan now.[115]

The diminution in size of the fauns also reduced any potential threat value they may have held. William Mitcheson Timlin shows us a tiny faun crouched like a bird on a tree branch, observing a young woman seated below but of no possible sexual threat to her. Charles Sims' *Little Faun* of 1908 is seen as an excited child, prancing between the crockery on a table set up for a meal beneath an apple tree by the Edwardian family watching him.

---

114   Redon, *Les Septs Péchées Capitaux*: seven menus for the Pré Catelan farm, the Pavillon d'Armenonville and the Paris Café.

115   See too E. Nesbit's *Enchanted Castle* (1907), in which she portrays a statute of a faun as a boy with a pretty, laughing face.

The tendency towards the infantilisation of fauns and satyrs may seem surprising in isolation, but it probably should be related to a similar process affecting other mythological and supernatural beings. In parallel, fairies and mermaids were being feminised and miniaturised, giving rise to such creatures as the 'flower fairies' and the Little Mermaid of Hans Christian Andersen. The traditional otherness and threat of these beings was substantially reduced or even entirely eradicated, making them most fit for children's stories. This may be seen in illustrations created for editions of *Wind in the Willows*, for instance by Paul Branson (1913), Nancy Barnhart (1922) or by Michael Hague (1980), to name just a few. The earthy character of the god was downplayed, whilst his divinity might be made more apparent.

Further examples of the neutering of the species are to be found in the work of Arthur Rackham. In 1918 he was commissioned to illustrate a special edition by Heinemann's of Swinburne's collection of children's verse, *The Springtide of Life*. One plate, which has little relation to the actual text "summer's rose garlanded train", shows a couple of adult women and a child gathering rose blossoms in a garden trellis arbour. The flowers are actually being picked by a topless goddess and the group are assisted by three pointy eared elves in medieval style clothes and by a satyr, who carries a basket on his head. This good-natured little fellow is skipping with delight, even though he has been reduced to a mere horticultural servant. In a second, extra plate for the book, a Pan figure with reed pipes sits beneath a gnarled old tree, instructing a group of small, naked boys – one of whom seems to be an elf and a second a faun. They are captivated by whatever Pan is telling them. In Rackham's vision, he has become a patient pedagogue – hardly the inspirer of panics.

These charming and harmless scenes notwithstanding, the mystery and potential weirdness of Pan did not disappear entirely. In *Before the Garden Statue* by Belgian artist Charles Joseph Watelet (1867–1954), a naked young woman clasps the face of a marble satire in an adoring way, as if about to kiss him. Her gesture is both devotional as well as sexual (given her nudity) and suggests strange rites without telling us much more. A similar mood is created in a picture by comic book illustrator John Allen St John. In the *Ancient Rites of Pan*, from *Fate Magazine,* September 1950 (see earlier), a satyr carries a naked girl on his shoulders; they stand before a giant statue of a goat god and the girl ecstatically raises a bunch of grapes to her mouth.

Finally, Austin Osman Spare (1886–1956), the occult writer and artist, envisioned bestial and unsettling fauns that seem to derive from the nightmare stories of Arthur Machen. In 1911 his illustration the *Senseless Seven* showed him surrounded by goats and satyrs. Spare also designed book plates on commission that depicted ancient shrines and the worship of Pan and, during the 1930s, he developed a portrait style that he called 'satyrisation,' in which his male subjects were subtly transformed with little beards and slightly pointed, fairy ears. Spare kept alive the true cult of Pan, with all its undercurrents of mystery and animal sexuality.

PAN IN SCULPTURE

The representation of Pan in oils was, in a sense, an innovation of the Renaissance, in that almost no pictorial representations of the god survived from antiquity. Sculpture was another matter, however, and models existed for later artists to imitate.[116] Indeed, Beatrice Irwin in her poem *Harmony,* on the sculptor Auguste Rodin, went as far as to say that he had "roused the God from his immortal sleep" when he cast the pipes of Pan.[117]

The French sculptor, Claude Michel Clodion (1738–1814) is particularly noted for his marble and terracotta studies of satyrs and nymphs. His iconography was very consistent – and quite faithful to its classical inspiration. *The Intoxication of Wine* of about 1780–90, for example, shows a goat legged satyr in the embrace of a nubile nymph. She is girlish and petite; he is more rugged and coarse. Clodion produced numerous similar pairings, sometimes with female bacchantes, sometimes eating grapes rather than drinking wine.

Comparable images continued to be created by followers of Clodion throughout the nineteenth and into the twentieth century, for example Albert-Ernest Carrier-Belleuse (1824–1887) and Edward Francis McCartan, whose *Nymph and Satyr* of 1920 features a satyr who could come straight from a painting by Böcklin, or even a Greek original, whilst the girl sports a fashionable flapper hairstyle of the period. German sculptor Reinhold Begas provided an interesting variation upon the familiar subjects when, in 1857, he carved *Pan Comforting Psyche*, a pairing surprisingly infrequently tackled by any artist.

French artist Theodore Gericault (1791–1824) produced a variety of images of sexual violence, amongst which are two versions of a *Nymph Attacked by a Satyr,* which are dated to

---

116 Amongst the most famous classical sculptures are Praxiteles' *Faun,* the *Dancing Faun* in the Lateran, the *Sleeping Faun, Drunken Faun* and *Faun and Bacchus* in Naples and the *Sleeping Satyr* in the Altepinakothek in Munich.

117 Irwin, 'Harmony' in *Pagan Trinity,* 1912; see also the poem *Eleusines.*

THE GREAT GOD PAN

between 1817 and 1820. The contact between the two is very obviously not consensual, with the nymph struggling to escape the clutches of the male and her mouth open wide in a scream. Another small bronze by Gericault that is often described as *Jupiter and Antiope* depicts a comparable, but slightly less forceful scene: the satyr bends in close to the nymph's face, or breasts, and she strains to turn her head away from him. The artist also drew a number of brush and chalk sketches depicting comparable scenes of unwanted attention.

Strongly recalling the work of Lossow is a small bronze by twentieth century Australian sculptor Rayner Hoff. *Faun and Nymph* shows the pair engaged in athletic and, presumably, passionate sexual intercourse – a slightly more decent modern version of the famous antique figures of Pan copulating with a goat.

CONTEMPORARY PAN

Images of Pan are still produced, even today. Serb Dragoslav Andrin has painted a *Faun and Nymph* in which the male is roughly molesting the female; Isaac Uribe has returned to the *Prelude to the Afternoon of the Faun* for inspiration (see later) and German Oleksii Gnievyshev has created a Pan with impressively curving ram's horns, an image possibly inspired by Schwabe's.

These images are quite conventional and fit within the classic traditions. British faery artist Brian Froud has drawn a subtly different goat-god, whom he called Poetic Pan. Like faeries, this Pan can materialise in many different places and, if humans come into contact with him, he will arouse in them erotic impulses, abandonment to poetic emotions and intense feelings of spiritual connection to nature." Froud warns us, however, to take care, "for his influence is overwhelming." This vision combines elements of the Greek god with newer perceptions that unite Pan with elementals, nature spirits and the environmental Pan of Robert Ogilvie Crombie.[118]

Most of these depictions are connected to, but perhaps not directly descended from, the work of earlier artists. Whereas those created their work within the tradition of classicism or symbolism, it is probable that post-war fantasy and sci-fi art has been a greater influence behind modern representations of the goat god.

---

118   Froud, *Good Faeries, Bad Faeries*, 1998,

CHAPTER 10

Pan in British Music

In 1876 French poet Stephane Mallarmé published *L'Apres Midi d'un Faune,* which was based on the story of Pan and Syrinx. It was intended as a dramatic 'eclogue' for performance on the stage and is a narrative spoken to himself by the faun. He describes two sleeping nymphs he has discovered and his frustrated love:

> "These nymphs I would make last.
> So rare
> Their rose lightness arches in the air,
> Torpid with tufted sleep.
> I loved: a dream?"

The poem proved remarkably inspirational for other artists. Pan and the nymphs were painted by Paul Ranson (1895), Pierre Bonnard in 1900 (one of a number of pictures featuring fauns) and by Ker Xavier Roussel in 1917– and again at later dates.

Mallarmé's poem also inspired numerous musical works, the most famous of which is the *Prélude à l'après-midi d'un faune* by Claude Debussy. This is a 'symphonic poem' and was first performed in December 1894. Debussy's ten-minute score was in turn adapted by Leon Bakst as a short ballet, the *Afternoon of a Faun*, which was choreographed and performed by Nijinsky in 1912. It was a highly eroticised performance that caused considerable scandal at the time. There are later interpretations, too, that were created in 1953 and 2006.

Other significant works of the period include Edward German's opera *Merrie England* (1902); Holst and Vaughan William's 1905 adaption of Ben Jonson's masque, *Pan's Anniversary*; The *Arcadians*, an operetta by Lionel Munckton and Howard Talbot that premiered in 1909; Ravel's 1912 ballet *Daphnis and Chloe*; Arthur Bliss' piece for clarinet and piano, *Pastoral* (1916); Alec Rowley's five movement piano composition *Festival of Pan* (1916–19); Frank Bridge's choral piece *Pan's Holiday*, composed in 1922, and several works by Sir Granville Bantock (1868–1946), including *The Great God Pan*, a 'choral ballet' composed in 1920, and a piano setting of Browning's *Pan and Luna* written in 1935. He also composed a *Pagan Symphony* (1928) which featured a dance of satyrs. Bantock's general interest in mystical or mythological themes can be discerned from the titles of many of his other works, which include *The Seal Woman*, described as a Celtic folk opera (1924), *Atalanta in Calydon*, a choral symphony based on Swinburne's poem (1912), *Pagan Chants* (1917), a *Celtic Symphony* of 1940, a *Celtic Poem* for cello and orchestra (1914) and *Thomas the Rhymer* (1946).

ARNOLD BAX AND PAGAN MUSIC

Arnold Bax (1883–1953) was a British composer for whom fairy and mythic themes were of major significance. From his time as a student at the Royal Academy of Music between 1900 and 1905 Bax was especially attracted to Ireland and Celtic folklore. His infatuation with Irish culture must be understood in the context of the heady *fin-de-siècle* ambience in which Bax's youthful imagination was nourished. The latest aesthetic fashions tended to favour anything sufficiently exotic as to afford a sharp contrast with common-place concerns and the humdrum practicalities of everyday life. Theosophy, Eastern mysticism, French Symbolism and the spiritual Celticism that was so much in vogue in the 1890s all contributed important strands to the young musician's development, while in the not too distant background lay the Pre-Raphaelite medievalism of Rossetti and William Morris. There was much talk at the time of neo-paganism and a strong interest in the occult. Undoubtedly, too, a large part of the general appeal was that over it all there hung a potent aura of decadent sexuality. To this can be added, particularly for a musician, Wagnerian music drama, the daring novelties of Strauss and, a decade or so later, the lavish splendour of the Russian ballet.

Early in his career, Bax composed many Celtic inspired pieces, including *A Celtic Song Cycle* of 1904, *Cathleen Ni Hoolihan* in 1905, and *Into the Twilight* of 1908. Several of these were heavily concerned with Irish myth and fairy themes, for example *In the Faëry Hills*. Despite the importance to Bax's music of ancient Irish myth and the mystic and fairy poetry of W B Yeats and Fiona Macleod, his influences were much broader and deeper. His works draw upon Irish and Arthurian myth, Scottish and Norse mythology, English folk tradition and the classical Greek legends

152

Bax's pagan Greek influences were channelled through 19th-century English literature such as Shelley's *Prometheus Unbound* and several works by Swinburne. The latter's recreation of this pagan world introduced a fresh element of ecstasy into English poetry which had an enormous appeal for Bax, whose own youthful outpourings, both musical and literary, are marked by an abundance of passionate intensity.

Another of his early scores, *The Happy Forest* (1914), bears a title taken from a prose-poem by Herbert Farjeon which was itself influenced by the *Idylls* of Theocritus, known as the 'father' of Greek pastoral poetry. Bax used Farjeon as a point of departure for painting a musical impression of an enchanted wood filled with 'the phantasmagoria of nature. Dryads, sylphs, fauns and satyrs abound – perhaps the goat-foot god may be there, but no man or woman'. The most important of his scores from this time, *Spring Fire* (1913), was based largely on the first chorus of Algernon Swinburne's *Atalanta in Calydon*, quotations from which appear at the head of each movement in the score. Completed at Tintagel and published in 1865, Swinburne's poetic drama retold the Greek myth of the killing of the wild Calydonian boar by a band of heroes that included the huntress Atalanta. Bax was concerned with the earthier, primitive aspects of Greek mythology: the erotic capers of sylvan demigods, the orgiastic frolics of the followers of Pan and Dionysus and the annual regeneration of nature.

Bax acknowledged the non-Celtic nature of the ideas behind *Spring Fire* and the other scores. He stated his view that 'the true ecstasy of spring' and the 'affirmation of life' are Hellenic concepts, foreign to the Celt: "Pan and Apollo, if ever they wandered so far from the Hesperidean garden as this icy Ierne, were banished at once in a reek of blood and mist and fire..."

153

Bax also wrote a solo piano work, *Nympholept*, which was completed in July 1912. Its title derives from Swinburne's 1894 evocation of the presence of Pan in a midday woodland (see earlier). Strictly, the term denotes one who suffers from nympholepsy (an obsession with a nymph) and, although on the manuscript Bax wrote that the piece concerned a person beguiled by the nymphs into the sunlight life of the wild-wood, when he described the work in 1951 he said instead that Swinburne had really been concerned with the panic induced by noonday silence in the woods.

These pagan scores date from the period just before the Great War, when – as we've already seen – there was a distinct artistic vogue for 'pagan' subjects such as these. Nijinsky's production of *L'après-midi d'un faune* had first been performed in 1912, and *The Rite of Spring* in 1913. Other classically inspired works of the period were Ravel's *Daphnis et Chloé* (1910), and Skryabin's *Prometheus* (1913). Thus, in creating the finest of his pre-war compositions, Bax was not only embodying his own 'adolescent dreams' but responding to a broader trend. However, the young composer's optimistic yearning for an imaginary Arcadian existence-'the ivory tower of my youth', as he called it in 1949– was soon to be swept away by the harsh realities of the Great War, the Easter Rising in Ireland and, on a more personal level, the disintegration of his marriage. Never again in his music was Bax to visit the world of classical antiquity, or to recapture the mood of unadulterated happiness and elation.

JOHN IRELAND AND ARTHUR MACHEN

For Arnold Bax, the love of myth and fairy lore was an intellectual matter; for fellow composer John Ireland it was real and physical, the product of sensation and experience. He once declared of himself: "I am a Pagan. A Pagan I was born and a Pagan I shall remain – that is the foundation of religion."

A key factor in Ireland's philosophy and music was the writing of Welsh novelist, Arthur Machen. The composer first came across Machen's work when he picked up a copy of *The House of Souls* at Preston railway station in 1906. He said that he instantly bought it and instantly loved it: its impact upon him was as important as had been reading De Quincey's *Confessions of an Opium Eater.*

Nearly thirty years later Ireland was to get to know Machen personally, but the author's world of fantasy and mystery had an immediate effect upon him. Machen's books have been described as a "catalyst" for Ireland, something which "infused" his compositions. He himself declared that his music could not be understood unless the listener had also read Machen's stories.

For Ireland, Machen had the status of a "seer." The composer's interest in magic and the unknown were ignited by the author's ideas and he shared with him a belief in the subconscious or 'racial memory,' the idea that through ancient sites such as barrows and standing stones he could connect to an ancient mysticism. At Chanctonbury Ring and Maiden Castle hillforts, for example, Ireland believed that he could still detect the early rites that had been performed there.

Ireland was especially fascinated by rituals and by the occult. He shared this, too, with Machen, who was a member of the Golden Dawn along with Yeats, Aleister Crowley, Bram Stoker and fellow fantasy novelist Algernon Blackwood. Ireland's particular devotion was to Pan. In 1952 he lamented that:

"The Great God Pan has departed from this planet, driven hence by the mastery of the material and the machine over mankind."

155

Ireland was not alone in this fascination of course. Pan had an aura of decadence and Ireland was definitely attracted to the god's darker side – the aspect celebrated by Machen.

Arthur Machen was not, of course, John Ireland's sole influence. Musically, he drew upon the spirit of Stravinsky's *Rite of Spring* and he also found John Brand's *Observations on Popular Antiquities,* a rich source of English fairy lore and folk tradition, an inspiration. The fairy author, Sylvia Townsend Warner, who happened also to be a relative of Machen, was a further influence, her concerns with physical and mental ecstasy matching Ireland's own. The composer had his own fairy experience as well, seeing some children-like figures at a ruined chapel on the South Downs. His piano concerto *Legend* was the product of this incident.

Ireland found Machen's novel *The Hill of Dreams* especially compelling and reckoned that it deserved a place in the 'literary hierarchy.' It never ceased to be a source of inspiration for him. As we saw earlier, it is the strange story of a young man who seems to come into contact with an ancient cult at an overgrown hill fort and who is eventually claimed by the satyrs and witches. The book probably helped shape Ireland's piano concerto, *Mai-Dun,* which takes its title from the name Thomas Hardy used for Maiden Castle.

One of the stories in Machen's *House of Souls* is the remarkable *White People,* an account by a young girl of her discovery of ancient magical rites in lost languages. She has encounters with mysterious white people (who may be fairies or nature spirits) and who play and dance and sing before her. Hidden mysteries, and the help they can give, are revealed to her by water nymphs and, finally, she discovers a lost statute of Pan – "the most wonderful sight I have ever seen," a secret thing in a secret wood. Ireland said that this haunting story had "astounding qualities" at which he "never ceased to marvel."

The story directly inspired three very short piano suites written in 1913 by Ireland, *Island Spell*, *Moon-Glade* and *Scarlet Ceremonies*, which he grouped together under the title *Decorations*. *Scarlet Ceremonies* took its title directly from a passage in *The White People*:

> "Then there are the ceremonies, which are all of them important, but some are more delightful than others: there are White Ceremonies, and the Green Ceremonies, and the Scarlet Ceremonies. The Scarlet Ceremonies are the best..."

Ireland's fascination with pagan ritual is also demonstrated by 1913's brief prelude for orchestra, *Forgotten Rite*, a composition that has been said to be permeated with Machen's notion of a "world beyond the walls," with the proximity of the supernatural, the theme that was tackled in his book *The Great God Pan* (see earlier). *Rite* was particularly inspired by the ancient megaliths of Guernsey, an island that Ireland described as being especially 'Machen-ish,' and evocative of Pan.

Conclusion

In late Victorian times Pan came to represent otherness – whether sexual, social or spiritual. Pan stood for the unresolved conflicts within British society and his dual – or even paradoxical – status was used to universalise and naturalise the issues he stood for – taking them out of a particular cultural or historical context and giving the anxieties they aroused general relevance. To some extent, Pan stood as a shorthand for freedom and hedonistic self-indulgence; nonetheless, he also marked a new attitude to nature – one that is still evolving today.

For most of those that mentioned him, Pan was a matter of cultural alignment rather than deep religious conviction. All the same, there was, for some around the turn of the last century, a genuine belief that paganism would emerge as a new religion. The frequency of pagan themes in literature and art must have made it seem more influential and widespread than was the case. This disappointment notwithstanding, paganism, and especially the cult of Pan, was a significant strand in culture and thinking during the closing decades of the nineteenth century and the first decades of the next. Various systems were advanced to make up for the waning faith in Christianity: science was one, theosophy and a more general mysticism were others. The exploration of these traditions in turn opened up new ways of thinking about the world. The cult of Pan didn't necessarily result in a new faith, but it laid the foundations for new perspectives that have had more impact, from Wicca to contemporary environmental activism.

More generally, Pan continues to pervade our culture, whether through the arts, literature or through film (for example, the 2006 Spanish film *Pan's Labyrinth* – originally and more correctly titled *El laberinto del fauno*, 'The Labyrinth of the Faun'). The goat god and his followers are still active within our collective psyche, stirring up strange visions that are both benign and malign.

The strength and the value of any myth or legend is its ability to evolve to speak to contemporary problems. Pan is a mutable god and he adapts to meet our most pressing needs. In late Victorian and Edwardian times, he was a vehicle for discussion of social (or rather sexual) reform. Today, we have made considerable advances in those areas and it is Pan's role as the shepherd and protector of the natural world that has come to the fore. In that function, we still require his guidance and his power.

Further Reading

Most of the books, short stories, poems and other texts cited in the course of this discussion are readily available online for readers to examine in full. For example, the site http://algernonblackwood. org/ has made nearly all his short stories available for free. Internet Archive, Hathi, Google Books and Gutenberg are other sites offering fully accessible novels and poetry collections.

Readers may also wish to examine the following:

Dingley, 'Meaning Everything: The Image of Pan at the Turn of the Century,' in *Twentieth Century Fantasists*, K. Filmer, 1992;

Freeman, N., *Nothing of the Wild Wood? Pan, Paganism and Spiritual Confusion, in Benson's 'The Man Who Went Too Far,'* 2005;

Hallett, J. R., *Paganism in England 1885–1914*, 2007;

Kip Baker, *Stories of Old Greece*, 1913;

Koumanoudi, A., 'The Great God Pan Never Dies!' in E. Almagor and L. Maurice, *The Reception of Ancient Virtues and Vices in Modern Popular Culture*, 2017;

Pettman, D., *After the Orgy – Towards a Politics of Exhaustion*, 2002;

Toland, E., *And Did Those Hooves: Pan and the Edwardians*, 2014.